A WOMAN'S HARDY GARDEN

BY
HELENA RUTHERFURD ELY

Foreword by Charles Elliott

A *HORTICULTURE* MAGAZINE GARDEN CLASSIC

THE LYONS PRESS

Dedication
TO THE BEST FRIEND OF MY GARDEN, WHO, WITH HEART
AND HANDS, HAS HELPED TO MAKE IT WHAT IT IS

Foreword copyright © 1999 by Charles Elliot
The special contents of this edition copyright © 1999 by
The Lyons Press

First published in 1903 by the Macmillan Company

First Lyons Press edition, 1999

Printed in the United States of America

10 9 8 7 6 5 4 3 2 1

Library of Congress Cataloging-in-Publication Data

Ely, Helena Rutherfurd, d. 1920.
  A woman's hardy garden / by Helena Rutherfurd Ely;
with illustrations from photographs taken in the author's
garden by C.F. Chandler.
    p.   cm.
  Originally published: New York: Macmillan Co., 1903.
  "A Horticulture magazine garden classic."
  Includes index.
  ISBN 1-55821-899-8 (pbk.)
  1. Flower gardening. 2. Perennials. 3. Landscape gardening.
I. Title.
SB405.E59   1999
635.9—dc21   99-11741
                                              CIP

A WOMAN'S
HARDY GARDEN

ROSE ARCH AND GARDEN WALK

FROM A WATER COLOR SKETCH BY

GEORGE B BARTHOLOMEW

PREFACE

THIS little book is only meant to tell briefly of a few shrubs, hardy perennials, biennials and annuals of simple culture. I send it forth, hoping that my readers may find within its pages some help to plant and make their gardens grow.

MEADOWBURN FARM
October, 1902

FOREWORD

WHEN Helena Rutherfurd Ely (1858–1920) published *A Woman's Hardy Garden,* in 1903, she was nearly fifty years old. It was her first book. But then she had never had any intention of becoming an author. Until that time her life had revolved, as with so many comfortably well-off American ladies, around family and children and garden. She was married to a prominent New York lawyer, with two houses to maintain—the Manhattan townhouse plus a suburban estate, Meadowburn Farm in Sussex County, New Jersey—and had an annual schedule calling for six months' residence in each, so writing books came a long way down Ely's list. But as she remarks in her introduction, "through trials and tribulations and hardly learned patience, I have gained some of the secrets of many of our best hardy flowering plants and shrubs . . . it has long been in my mind to write down what I know of hardy gardening, that other women might be helped to avoid the experiments and mistakes I have made, which only served to cause delay."

In these more enlightened times, her focus on "women" and "woman gardeners" may strike an off note. The fact is, however, that a hundred years ago—particularly in the United States—flower gardening was widely regarded as an activity mainly for women. Almost all of the serious how-to books, both before and after *A Woman's Hardy Garden,* were written by women. And women were responsible for many of the most distinguished gardens in existence around the turn of the century, especially in gardening's New England heartland. While this had some historical logic behind it (the fashion was turning to old-timey "grandmothers' gardens" of the cottage-garden type), the preeminence of women in the field is still remarkable.

Mrs. Ely saw her book as a straightforward and highly utilitarian handbook, which indeed it was and still remains. A reviewer in the *New York Tribune* praised her as "the wisest and most winning teacher of the fascinating art of gardening that we have met in modern print," while the *Times* remarked that she provided "much information to be appreciated only by those who have raised a healthy garden by the slow teaching of personal experience." It is true that the book radiates firsthand knowledge on subjects ranging from the best shrubs for shade to how to prepare and use a seedbed. But it also should be recognized as an influential part of a more general shift in garden design, whose effects are still with us. Through much of the nineteenth century, bedding-out reigned supreme. Victorian taste called for beds cut into geometrical shapes or curlicues and filled with brightly colored annuals or tender perennials arranged to form patterns. Labor-intensive, unromantic, and deliberately artificial, bedding-out scorned the use of such familiar old favorites as foxgloves or sunflowers or most of the other staples of the cottage garden. A memoir by her daughter notes that Mrs. Ely's own first garden after her marriage consisted of geometrical beds of annuals. In the 1880s and 1890s, with the advent of William Robertson and especially Gertrude Jekyll (whose gardening books achieved wide circulation) in England, and in America a new fascination with colonial houses and gardens, all this changed. "The taste for old-fashioned gardens is revived," wrote the great botanist Charles Sprague Sargent in 1895. "There is a fresh call for the perennials and annuals which enlivened the borders of long ago."

It was in this context that Helena Rutherfurd Ely produced *A Woman's Hardy Garden* and its two successors, *Another Hardy Garden Book* (1905) and *The Practical Flower Garden* (1911). Her daughter's memoir recalls how, traveling around the countryside, Ely was "charmed" by the hardy flowers grown in the dooryards of New Jersey farmhouses, and started her own borders with plants, roots, and seeds "begged from her friends among the farmers' wives." By the time she began writing, a full-scale movement was underway. "Even as the mahogany of our grandfathers is now brought forth from garrets and unused rooms, and antiquity shops and farm-houses are searched for the good old-time furniture," she comments, "so we are learning to take the old gardens for our models, and the old-fashioned flowers to fill our borders." Delphiniums, peonies, columbines, canterbury bells, phloxes, sweet williams—such are the "old-fashioned flowers" that she recommended and wrote about. Fortunately they are the flowers that many of us—men as well as women—still want to grow.

It could be argued (and was, at the time) that Mrs. Ely was not really addressing ordinary gardeners, but only those rich enough to have a staff to do the hard work. The garden historian May Brawley Hill has tracked down a report by the publisher's reader of *A Woman's Hardy Garden,* who found it "valuable to the novice" but complained that "the author is affluent—

those who will use the book are not likely to be."
This brought an angry rejoinder from Mrs. Ely.
Still, anyone with a backache from some serious double digging or manure spreading can't
help but notice the occasional mention of "one
of the men" or "one of our gardeners," or feel a
sting of envy when she descants upon the difficulty of hiring a professional who combines
sobriety with skill. On the other hand, quite
apart from its vividly practical content, the his-
tory of this book demonstrates how it was
welcomed by a vast number of non-affluent
American gardeners. Reprinted no fewer than
ten times within four years of its first publica-
tion, it stayed continually in print for nearly
thirty years, and was reprinted from time to
time thereafter. Hundreds of gardens were
based upon its precepts, thousands of gardeners inspired to make use of dependable native
species in plantings that were essentially natural and offered a sequence of bloom. In its own
modest way, it was revolutionary.

—Charles Elliott
London, 1999

TABLE OF CONTENTS

INTRODUCTION

CHAPTER I

INTRODUCTION

LOVE of flowers and all things green and growing is with many men and women a passion so strong that it often seems to be a sort of primal instinct, coming down through generation after generation, from the first man who was put into a garden "to dress it and to keep it." People whose lives, and those of their parents before them, have been spent in dingy tenements, and whose only garden is a rickety soap-box high up on a fire-escape, share this love, which must have a plant to tend, with those whose gardens cover acres and whose plants have been gathered from all the countries of the world. How often in summer, when called to town, and when driving through the squalid streets to the ferries or riding on the elevated road, one sees these gardens of the poor. Sometimes they are only a Geranium or two, or the gay Petunia. Often a tall Sun-flower, or a Tomato plant red with fruit. These efforts tell of the love for the growing things, and of the care that makes them live and blossom against all odds. One feels a thrill of sympathy with the owners of the plants, and wishes that some day their lot may be cast in happier places, where they too may have gardens to tend.

It has always seemed to me that the punishment of the first gardener and his wife was the bitterest of all. To have lived always in a garden "where grew every tree pleasant to the sight and good for food," to have known no other place, and then to have been driven forth into the great world without hope of returning! Oh! Eve, had you not desired wisdom, your happy children might still be tilling the soil of that blessed Eden. The first woman longed for knowledge, as do her daughters of to-day. When the serpent said that eating of the forbidden fruit would make them "as gods," what wonder that Eve forgot the threatening command to leave untouched the Tree of Life, and, burning to be "wise," ate of the fateful apple and gave it to her Adam? And then, to leave the lovely place at the loveliest of all times in a garden, the cool of the day! Faint sunset hues tinting the sky, the night breeze gently stirring the trees, Lilies and Roses giving their sweetest perfume, brilliant Venus mounting her accustomed path, while the sleepy twitter of the birds alone breaks the silence. Then the voice of wrath, the Cherubim, the turning flaming sword!

Through trials and tribulations and hardly learned patience, I have gained some of the secrets of many of our best hardy flowering plants and shrubs. Many friends have asked me to tell them when to plant or transplant, when to sow this or that seed, and how to prepare the beds and borders; in fact, this has occurred so often that it has long been in my mind to write down what I know of hardy gardening, that other women might be helped to avoid the experiments and mistakes I have made, which only served to cause delay.

But just this "please write it down," while sounding so easy and presenting to the mind such a fascinating picture of a well-printed, well-illustrated and prettily bound book on the garden, is quite a different matter to one who has never written. When you diffidently try to explain the chaos in your brain, family and friends say, "Oh! never mind; just begin." That often-quoted "*premier pas!*"

To-day is the first snow-storm of the winter, and, while sitting by the fireside, my thoughts are so upon my garden, wondering if this or that will survive, and whether the plants remember me, that it seems as though to-day I could try that first dreaded step.

Living all my life, six months and sometimes more of each year, in the country,—real country on a large farm, —I have from childhood been more than ordinarily interested in gardening. Surrounded from babyhood with

6

horses and dogs, my time as a little girl was spent out of doors, and whenever I could escape from a patient governess, whose eyes early became sad because of the difficulties of her task, I was either riding a black pony of wicked temper, or was to be found in a lovely garden with tall Arborvitæ hedges and Box-edged walks, in the company of an old gardener, one of my very best friends, who for twenty years ruled master and mistress, as well as garden and graperies. Under this old gardener, I learned, even as a child, to bud Roses and fruit trees, and watched the transplanting of seedlings and making of slips; watched, too, the trimming of grape-vines, fruit trees and shrubs; so that while still very young I knew more than many an older person of practical garden work. Then, as I grew older, the interests of a gay girl, and, later, the claims of early married life and the care of two fat and fascinating babies, absorbed my time and thoughts to the exclusion of the garden. But as the babies grew into a big boy and girl, the garden came to the front again, and, for more than a dozen years now, it has been my joy,—joy in summer when watching the growth and bloom, and joy in winter when planning for the spring and summer's work. There is pleasure even in making lists, reading catalogues of plants and seeds, and wondering whether this year my flowers will be like the pictured ones, and always, in imagination, seeing how the sleeping plants will look when robed in fullest beauty.

HARDY GARDENING AND THE PREPARATION OF THE SOIL

CHAPTER II

HARDY GARDENING AND THE PREPARATION
OF THE SOIL

IT has not been all success. I have had to
learn the soil and the location best suited
to each plant; to know when each bloomed
and which lived best together. Mine is a
garden of bulbs, annuals, biennials and hardy
perennials; in addition to which there are
Cannas, Dahlias and Gladioli, whose roots
can be stored, through the winter, in a cellar.
All the rest of the garden goes gently to
sleep in the autumn, is well covered up
about Thanksgiving time, and slumbers
quietly through the winter; until, with the first
spring rains and sunny days, the plants seem
fairly to bound into life again, and the never-
ceasing miracle of nature is repeated before
our wondering eyes.

11

I have no glass on my place, not even a cold-frame or hot-bed. Everything is raised in the open ground, except the few bedding plants mentioned whose roots are stored through the winter. Therefore, mine can truly be called a hardy garden, and is the only one I know at all approaching it in size and quantity of flowers raised, where similar conditions exist.

I have observed that, with few exceptions, the least success with hardy perennials is found in the gardens of those of my friends whose gardeners are supposed to be the best, because paid the most. These men will grow wonderful Roses, Orchids, Carnations, Grapes, etc., under glass, and will often have fine displays of Rhododendrons. But to most of them the perennial or biennial plant, the old friend blossoming in the same place year after year, is an object unworthy of cultivation. Their souls rejoice in the bedding-out plant, which must be yearly renewed, and which is beautiful for so short a time, dying

12

with the early frost. I was astounded last summer on visiting several fine places, where the gardeners were considered masters of their art, to see the poor planting of perennials and annuals. I recall particularly two Italian gardens, perfectly laid out by landscape gardeners, but which amounted to nothing because the planting was insufficient,—here a Phlox, there a Lily, then a Rose, with perhaps a Larkspur or a Marigold, all rigidly set out in single plants far apart, with nothing in masses, and no colour effects.

To attain success in growth, as well as in effect, plants must be so closely set that when they are developed no ground is to be seen. If so placed, their foliage shades the earth, and moisture is retained. In a border planted in this way, individual plants are far finer than those which, when grown, are six inches or a foot apart.

First of all in gardening, comes the preparation of the soil. Give the plants the food they need and plenty of water, and the blessed sunlight will do the rest. It is wonderful what can be done with a small space, and how from April to November there can always be a mass of bloom. I know of one woman's garden, in a small country town,—house and ground only covering a lot hardly fifty by one hundred feet,—where, with the help of a man to work for her one day in the week and perhaps for a week each spring and fall, she raises immense quantities of flowers, both perennials and annuals. For six months of the year she has always a dozen vases full in the house, and plenty to give away. More than half the time her little garden supplies flowers for the church, while others in the same village owning large places and employing several men "have really no flowers."

I remember returning once from a two weeks' trip, to find that my entire crop of Asters had been destroyed by a beetle. It was a horrid black creature about an inch long, which appeared in swarms, devoured all the plants and then disappeared, touching nothing else. Such a thing had never before happened in my garden. One of the men had sprayed them with both slug-shot and kerosene emulsion to no effect,—and so no Asters. My friend with the little garden heard me bemoaning my loss, and the next day sent me, over the five intervening miles, a hamper —almost a small clothes-basket—full of the beautiful things. It quite took my breath away. I wondered how she could do it, and thought she must have given me every one she had. Yet, upon driving over in hot haste to pour out thanks and regrets, lo! there were Asters all a-blow in such quantities in her garden that it seemed as if none had been gathered.

Except by the sea-coast, our dry summers, with burning sun and, in many places, frequent absence of dew, are terribly hard on a garden; but with deep, rich soil, and plenty of water and proper care, it will yield an almost tropical growth. Therefore, whenever a bed or border is to be made, make it right. Unless one is willing to take the trouble properly to prepare the ground, there is no use in expecting success in gardening. I have but one rule: stake out the bed, and then dig out the entire space two feet in depth. Often stones will be found requiring the strength and labor of several men, with crowbars and levers, to remove them; often there will be rocks that require blasting. Stones and earth being all removed, put a foot of well-rotted manure in the bottom; then fill up with alternate layers, about four inches each, of the top soil, taken out of the first foot dug up, and of manure. Fill the bed or border very full, as it will sink with the disintegration of the manure. Finish off the top with three inches of soil. Then it is ready for planting. If the natural soil is stiff or clayey, put it in a heap and mix with one-fourth sand, to lighten it, before returning to the bed. Thus prepared, it will retain moisture, and not pack and become hard.

16

LAYING OUT A GARDEN AND BORDERS AROUND THE HOUSE

CHAPTER III

LAYING OUT A GARDEN AND BORDERS AROUND
THE HOUSE

PERPLEXITIES assail a would-be gardener on every side, from the day it is decided to start a garden. The most attractive books on the subject are English; and yet, beyond the suggestions for planting, and the designs given in the illustrations, not much help is to be derived in this latitude from following their directions. In England the climate, which is without great extremes of heat and cold, and the frequent rains, with the soft moist atmosphere, not only enable the English gardener to accomplish what would be impossible for us, but permit him to grow certain flowers out of doors that here must be housed in the winter. Daffodils and Narcissi bloom in England, near the

19

coast, at the end of February and early in March,—Lilies-of-the-Valley in March. Many Roses live out of doors that would perish here during our winters. Gardening operations are begun there much earlier than in this part, at least, of the United States, and many of the methods for culture differ from those employed here. In England there is excess of moisture; therefore, care in securing good drainage is essential, while here, except in low places near streams, special provision for drainage is rarely necessary. It is more important to have a deep, rich preparation of the soil, so that plants may not be dried out. A serious part of the gardener's work during the average summer consists in judicious watering of the garden.

One writer will say that this or that plant should have sun, another that it does best in the shade. One advocates a rich soil, another a light sandy soil; so that after all, in gardening, as in all else in life, experience is the best teacher, either your own or that of others who have already been successful under similar conditions.

A garden is almost sure to be gradually increased in size, and its capacity limited only by the grounds of the owner and his pocket-book. The possibilities and capabilities of a couple of acres are great, and will give the owner unlimited pleasure and occupation.

Individuality is one of the most marked of American characteristics; hence, in making a place, whether it is big or little, the tastes and individuality of the owner will generally direct his efforts, and no hard and fast rules can be given.

In starting a garden, the first question, of course, is where to plant. If you are a beginner in the art, and the place is new and large, go to a good landscape gardener and let him give advice and make you a plan. But don't follow it; at least not at once, nor all at one time. Live there for a while, until you yourself begin to feel what you want, and where you want it. See all the gardens and places you can, and then, when you know what you want, or think you do, start in.

The relation of house to grounds must always be borne in mind, and simplicity in grounds should correspond with that of the house. A craze for Italian gardens is seizing upon people generally, regardless of the archi-tecture of their houses. To my mind, an Italian garden, with its balustrades, terraces, fountains and statues, is as inappropriate for surrounding a colonial or an ordinary country house as would be a Louis XV drawing-room in a farm-house.

What is beautiful in one place becomes incongruous and ridiculous in another. Not long ago, a woman making an afternoon visit asked me to show her the gardens. Daintily balancing herself upon slippers with the highest possible heels, clad in a costume appropriate only for a fête at Newport, she strolled about. She thought it all "quite lovely" and "really, very nice," but, at least ten times, while making the tour, wondered "Why in the world don't you have an Italian garden?" No explanation of the lack of taste that such a garden would indicate in connection with the house, had any effect. The simple, formal gardens of a hundred years ago, with Box-edged paths, borders and regular Box-edged beds, are always beautiful, never become tiresome, and have the additional merit of being appropriate either to the fine country-place or the simple cottage.

For a small plot of ground, like the one before mentioned, the plan of which is on page 24, the matter is simple, because of the natural limitations. I love to see a house bedded, as it were, in flowers. This is par-ticularly suitable for the usual American country house, colonial in style, or low and rambling. Make a bed perhaps four feet wide along three sides of the house,—south, east and west. Close against the house plant the vines. Every one has an individual taste in vines,—more so, perhaps, than in any other ornamental growth. If the house be of stone,

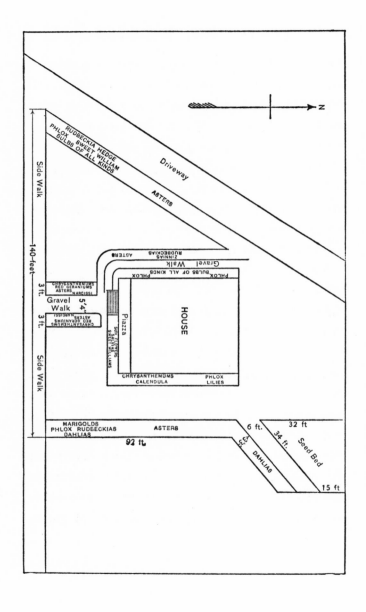

and the climate not too severe, nothing is more beautiful than the English Ivy. It flourishes as far north as Princeton, New Jersey. I have never grown it, fearing it would be winter-killed.

Ampelopsis Veitchii, sometimes called Boston Ivy, grows rapidly, clinging closely to the wall and turning a dark red in the autumn, and is most satisfactory.

The Virginia Creeper, and the Trumpet Creeper, with its scarlet flowers, are both beautiful, perfectly hardy, and of rapid growth. All of these vines cling to stone and wood, and, beyond a little help for the first two or three feet, need not be fastened to the house. Care must be taken to prevent the vines growing too thickly to admit sun and air to the house.

If the house be of wood, the question of repainting must be considered. Both the White and the Purple Wistaria, which can be twined about heavy wire and fastened at the eaves, Rambler Roses and Honeysuckles may be grown. They can be laid down, to permit painting. But, if the house be of wood and well covered with vines, put off the evil day of painting until it can be deferred no longer, and then have it done early in November. Never, never permit it to be done in the spring, or before November, unless you would take the risk of killing the vines or of losing at least a season's growth. The house surrounded by my gardens is colonial, something over a hundred and fifty years old, stern and very simple. Tall locusts, towering above the roof, and vines that cover it from ground to eaves, have taken away its otherwise puritanical and somewhat uncompromising aspect. These vines are mostly the ordinary Virginia Creeper, which I had dug from the woods and planted when the first fat baby was two months old. Now their main trunks are, in places, as large as my arm. They have never been laid down. Whenever the house has been repainted, I have been constantly by, and admonished the men to gently lift the heavy branches while painting under them, and not to paint the light tendrils. When the master-painter has remonstrated, that it was not a "good job" and took three times as long as if the vines were laid down, my reply has been, that "three times" was nothing in comparison with the years it had taken to grow them, and that stunting or killing the vines could never be a "good job."

Among the creepers are the Crimson Rambler Rose and the Honeysuckle. In three years the Roses have grown above the second-story windows.

Clematis paniculata, with its delicate foliage and mass of starry bloom in early autumn, is particularly good to plant by veranda posts in connection with other vines. It grows luxuriantly and is absolutely hardy. The large white-flowered Henryi and purple-flowered Jackmani Clematis, though of slow growth, should always have a place, either about a veranda, a summer-house or a trellis, for the sake of their beautiful flowers.

While waiting for the hardy vines to make their first year's growth, the seeds of the Japanese Morning-Glory, the Japanese Moon-Flower and *Cobœa scandens* may be planted. All of these will grow at least ten feet in a summer, and cover the bare places. But I would not advise sowing them among the hardy vines, except the first summer. In their luxuriance they may suffocate the Roses and Clematis. The seeds of the Moon-Flower must be soaked in hot water, and left over night, before sowing. So much for the vines about a house.

In front of the vines, and on the south side in the same bed, plant masses of Hollyhocks, from eight to twelve in a bunch, and Rudbeckia in bunches of not more than five, as they grow so large. Hollyhocks and Rudbeckias plant two feet apart; they will grow to a solid mass. In front of these, again, put a clump of Phloxes, seven in a bunch, and Larkspur, *Delphinium formosum* being the best. On either side of the Delphinium have clumps of about a dozen *Lilium candidum*, which bloom at the same time. Edge the border with Sweet Williams, three kinds only,—white, pink and dark scarlet.

I should not advise making all the borders around a house alike. The easterly one will be most lovely if planted with tall ferns or brakes, taken from near some stream in early April, before they begin to grow. These will become about four feet high if you get good roots and keep them wet. Plant in among them everywhere Auratum Lilies, and you will have a border that will fill your heart with joy. On the north side of the house it is not possible to have much success with vines, as they need the sun. They will grow, but not with great luxuriance. Here plant two rows of the common *Rhododendron maximum*, which grows in our woods. I crave pardon for calling it "common," since none that grows is more beautiful.

In front of these plant ferns of all kinds from the woods, and edge the border with

Columbines. If these Rhododendrons do not grow in your vicinity, they can be ordered from a florist. In the hills, about five miles from us, acres of them grow wild, and twice a year I send my men with wagons to dig them up. They stand transplanting perfectly if care is taken to get all the roots, which is not difficult, as they do not grow deep. Keep them quite wet for a week after planting, and never let them get very dry. A good plan is to mulch them in early June to the depth of six inches or more with the clippings of the lawn grass, or with old manure. When once well rooted, the Rhododendrons will last a lifetime. They seem to bear transplanting at any season. Some think they do best if taken when in full bloom. I have always done this in April or late October, and, of a wagon-load transplanted last October, all have lived. Many of these were like trees, quite eight feet tall and too large to be satisfactory about the house, so they were set among the evergreens in a shrubbery.

In cold localities, where the thermometer in winter falls below zero, Rhododendrons should be mulched with stable litter or leaves to the depth of one foot, after the ground has frozen. They should also have some protection from the winter sun, which can be easily given them by setting evergreen boughs of any kind into the ground here and there among them. Rhododendrons are as likely to be killed by alternate freezing and thawing of the ground in winter as by summer drought.

The lovely *Azalea mollis*, and many beautiful varieties of imported Rhododendrons, are usually described as "hardy," but I cannot recommend them to those who live where the winters are severe. In such places their growth is very slow, and many perish.

Maidenhair, the most beautiful of the hardy ferns, is to be found in quantities in many of our woods, particularly those covering hillsides. Their favorite spot is along the edges of mountain brooks. I know such a hillside,

31

where Maidenhair Ferns are superb. But nothing would induce me to venture there again, since I have been told it was infested with rattlesnakes, and that the woodchoppers kill a number of them every year. This fact, too, gives me scruples about sending the men to dig them up, although it is an awful temptation.

All ferns should be transplanted late in the autumn, or very early in the spring before the fronds are started, as they are very easily broken. This is particularly the case with ferns from wet places. When planted on the east or north side of a house, the tall ones at the back, and Maidenhair and other low varieties in front, they make a beautiful bank of cool green. They must be kept moist, however, to be successful, and in dry weather require a daily soaking.

The Cardinal Flower, whose natural haunt is along the banks of streams, and whose spikes are of the most beautiful red, can also be safely transplanted, and will bloom in deep, rich soil equally well in shade or sun and will be very effective among the Ferns. About the end of November, after cutting the dead stalks, cover each plant with a piece of sod, laid grass-side down. Remove this the first of April, and the little sprouts will soon appear above the ground. Cardinal Flowers bloom for nearly a month —during the last two weeks of August and first two weeks of September.

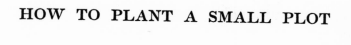

HOW TO PLANT A SMALL PLOT

CHAPTER IV

HOW TO PLANT A SMALL PLOT

I AM frequently surprised to hear people say, "Oh, a flower garden is very nice, but such a trouble!" I have heard this expression several times from friends who employ a number of men and have large places with extensive lawns, shrubberies and vegetable gardens, but without flowers, except, perhaps, a few annuals growing among the vegetables.

Yet no one is indifferent to the beauty of a garden, or unobservant of the improvement which even a few flowers can make around the humblest cottage. Think of the pretty thatched cottages one sees everywhere in England and France, covered to the eaves with Roses and Clematis, and surrounded by flowers growing wherever they can find root in the tiny gardens. Yet all this is the result of only a half hour's daily care after the long day's work is done.

One should begin with a few plants—perhaps a dozen only—and the "trouble" will soon become a delight, unless one is devoid of all love for flowers.

Whenever I hear remarks on the "trouble" of a flower garden, I think of those peasant homes, and also of a little plot grown and cared for by a certain tenant farmer's wife I know. She has six children, and must cook and bake and clean for four men in addition; yet, some time every day, she finds a few minutes to tend her flowers. She has a border along the fence four by fifty feet, filled with perennials; a border across the front of her house with Phlox and Funkias, and a couple of beds with Asters, Poppies, Balsams, Portulaca and Pinks. The perennials were given her, a few at a time. She separated the roots, saved the seeds to raise others, and has been able in this way to increase her borders. The seeds of the few annuals she buys do not cost more than a dollar a year. Thus, for a trifling expenditure and a short time every day, this woman makes her humble surroundings beautiful, while her soul finds an object upon which to expend its love of beauty, and her thoughts have a respite from the daily cares of life.

Many people have the mistaken idea that a flower garden, however small, is an expensive luxury, and are so convinced of this, that they never venture any attempt at gardening, and pass their lives knowing nothing of its pleasures.

Let us suppose some one is starting a suburban home in a simple way, and see how flowers can be had for many months at small cost. If one has a place in a town or village, the plot of ground not over fifty by two hundred feet, still the possibilities are great, and the owner can easily gather flowers for herself and her friends from April until mid-November. A house or cottage on such a piece of ground generally stands back from twenty to fifty feet, with a gravel or flagged walk running to the street. If the owner be a beginner in gardening and expects to do most of the work herself, let her commence with a few plants in a small space. As the plants thrive and become beautiful, the care of them will give an added pleasure to life, and, little by little, the beds and borders can be increased.

In beginning to plant a small plot, the most natural place first is a border, say two feet wide, on either side of the walk leading from the house to the street. Have these borders dug out and made properly. Then, if the owner wishes to see them continually abloom, bulbs must be planted, to give the early spring flowers. Tulips can be had for eighty cents a hundred, *Narcissus Poeticus* for sixty-five cents a hundred, and Yellow Daffodils for one dollar and twenty-five cents a hundred. Hyacinths are more expensive, and cost from four dollars a hundred up. If a

hundred each of the Tulips, Narcissi, Hyacinths and Daffodils were planted they would
make the borders lovely from early in April
until late in May. The Daffodils will bloom
first, then the Hyacinths, followed by the
Narcissi, and the Tulips last, if care is taken
to buy a late variety.

There should certainly be three or four
Peonies in the borders,— pink, white, and
dark red ; good roots of these can be had for
about thirty-five cents each. Once planted,
they should not be disturbed for years; and,
although the first season they may not yield
more than two or three blossoms, in each
succeeding year the flowers will increase in
number. A friend told me, not long ago,
that she had counted sixty blossoms upon
each of several of her plants.

There should also be at least a dozen
Columbines (Aquilegias) to bloom the end
of May and the first of June. The roots of
these can be bought for a dollar and a half
a dozen, or they can be raised from seed ; in

the latter case, however, they would not bloom until the second year, being perennials.

No border can be complete without Delphiniums (Larkspur). Good-sized roots of the *Delphinium formosum*, lovely dark blue, are a dollar and twenty-five cents a dozen. *Formosum Cœlistina*, the light blue variety, is two dollars and a half a dozen. Then, of course, there must be other perennials,— Phlox, at least a dozen plants in the different colours, which will cost a dollar and a half.

A few Lilies will add greatly to the beauty of the borders. Tiger Lilies, which are only sixty cents a dozen; Auratums, which can be had from eighty-five cents a dozen up, according to the size of the bulbs; *Speciosum rubrum* from eighty-five cents a dozen up, and Candidums, or Madonna Lilies, a dollar and a half a dozen. German Iris, a dollar a dozen, and Japanese Iris, at a dollar and a quarter a dozen, should also have a place.

Excellent Gladioli can be bought for a dollar and fifty cents a hundred, and these will be most satisfactory if planted in the border about May fifteenth in groups of six to ten.

A dozen Chrysanthemums of the hardiest varieties to be obtained, and costing a dollar and a half a dozen, will, with the other plants mentioned, about fill two borders two feet wide by thirty long. It would also be well to sow the seeds of some Calendulas, Nasturtiums and Asters wherever there may be a vacant place. Or better, perhaps, sow the seeds in boxes in mid-April, and transplant to the border the early part of June. The first cost will be the only expense for these borders, except in the case of the Auratum Lilies, which will die out in about three years, and of the few flower seeds. The only care needed is to keep the borders free from weeds, to stir the soil every week, and to water after sunset in dry weather.

It will be seen, from the following list, that such borders can easily be made and planted at a cost of less than thirty dollars. This can be reduced by omitting the Hyacinths. Directions for planting are given elsewhere.

	PRICE
Tulips	$0 80
Narcissi	65
Daffodils	1 25
Hyacinths	4 00
Peonies	1 40
Columbines	1 50
Delphinium Formosum	1 25
Delphinium Cœlestina	2 50
Phlox	1 50
Tiger Lilies	60
Auratum	85
Lilium rubrum	85
Lilium candidum	1 50
Japanese Iris	1 25
Iris Germanica	1 00
Chrysanthemums	1 50
Flower seeds	1 00
Three days' work, at $1.50 per day	4 50
Manure	1 50
Total	$29 40

HOW TO PLANT A SMALL PLOT

After a year or two, the owner of the cottage may want to increase the flower garden, and the next place to plant is close about the house. It is to be taken for granted that the house and piazzas have the proper gutters. This is necessary, of course, for the preservation of the house, and without gutters the drip from the eaves would be such that nothing could grow directly against the house.

The bed might be three feet wide and run across the front of the house on either side of the steps. The owner would probably wish to plant vines over the porch or piazza, in case it has not already been done. The best for this purpose are mentioned elsewhere.

Should the house front the south, east or west, nearly everything can be grown; but should it face the north, nothing but Ferns and Rhododendrons would be successful on the front. Dahlias of the Cactus variety, in different colours, could be planted at the back of the bed on one side of the steps. Get good-sized roots, plant them two feet apart. They will grow against the house like a tall hedge. If planted the third week in April quite deep, say eight inches, they will begin to bloom about the sixth of July, and continue to be covered with flowers until killed by frost. In front of the Dahlias, plant white Phlox. In front of the Phlox sow a row of *Centaurea* or Cornflowers, the Emperor William variety. These should be sown early in April, will begin to bloom by June tenth, and, if they are not allowed to go to seed, will blossom all summer. Sow in front of the Cornflowers, at the same time, a row of white Candytuft, of the Empress variety. This also will bloom continuously if the flowers are cut as soon as they wither. On the other side of the steps, at the back of the bed, plant Rudbeckia (Golden Glow) two feet apart. The roots should be bought and planted, preferably in October, otherwise as soon as the frost is out of the ground in the spring,

46

as they start very early. In front of the
Rudbeckias plant Cannas — the Tarrytown,
of most vivid scarlet hue, I have found the
best and freest-flowering of all. The roots
should be planted about May fifteenth.

On the edge of the bed, sow by April
fifteenth a row of salmon-pink Zinnias, and
when they are well up, thin out to six
inches apart. They begin to blossom when
very small, and will stand considerable frost.
The expense of these beds will be trifling.
Rudbeckias of the Golden Glow variety,
one dollar a dozen; the Tarrytown Canna,
two dollars and a half a dozen; Cactus
Dahlias, two dollars a dozen; Phlox, one
dollar and a half a dozen. The small quantity of flower seeds required will cost less
than a dollar. A man can easily make the
beds in three days. Therefore, the cost with
manure will be less than fifteen dollars.

After a hard frost has killed the tops,
the Dahlias, Cannas and Gladioli should be
taken up, the tops cut off, the roots well

dried, and then stored in a cellar that does not freeze. The Canna and Dahlia roots will have grown so large that they can be divided and it will be found that there are enough to plant, the following spring, nearly twice the space they occupied before.

It is impossible, if successful with the borders already planned, for the owner not to wish for more garden. She sees the neighbors' gardens with newly opened eyes; flowers and their treatment become an absorbing topic of conversation, and the exchange of plants a delightful transaction.

It will be seen that the next places to plant are along the boundary lines of the property. Even if one side only be laid out at a time, a large number of plants will be required. The owner will find great pleasure in raising as many of these herself as possible. To accomplish this, somewhere at the back of the place, a seed-bed should be made, and in April the seeds of perennials and annuals sown. The border must be made by September the twentieth and should be at least four feet wide. Either a hedge can be placed at the back of the border, or tall-growing flowering shrubs, such as white and purple Lilacs (not the Persian), Mock Oranges (Syringa), Deutzia and Roses of Sharon (Althea). These shrubs will grow about equally high, yield an abundance of flowers, the Altheas in August, the others in May or June, and in four or five years will form a complete screen from the neighboring grounds.

In front of the shrubs perennials can be planted, taller ones at the back, lower-growing ones in front, and annuals along the edge. Such a border, if from fifty to a hundred feet in length, will be a garden by itself. The plants will do best if closely set, and every vacant space filled in June with annuals. Weeds then have little chance to grow, and a short time every day will keep such a border in order. The border can be of any width from four to twelve feet, but

49

when more than four feet, the front edge should be made with irregular curves to avoid a stiff appearance.

Shrubs should be set out not later than October tenth, and, as they or the hedge would be at the back of the bed, the planting of them will not interfere with the perennials that have already been transplanted from the seed-bed. Hedges are so much more beautiful than any fence that ever was built that, in towns or villages where cattle are not allowed to run at large, hedges should, wherever possible, be used in place of fences.

To prepare the ground for a hedge, make a trench eighteen inches deep, put a good layer of well-rotted manure in the bottom and fill up with earth. When the hedge is planted give it a good top-dressing of manure, and continue this top-dressing, with a little bone-meal sown on the surface of the ground, every spring.

The best and hardiest evergreen hedge is of Hemlock Spruce. Plants of this can be bought for fifteen dollars a hundred, and should be set eighteen inches apart.

The Privet is a favorite hedge in this country. It keeps green until December, and leafs out early in the spring. It is hardy and of rapid growth. Good plants are six dollars a hundred, and should be planted a foot apart. Catalogues say that if planted in rich soil one foot apart, a hedge five feet high can be grown in three seasons. Common Privet is more hardy than California Privet. *Hydrangea paniculata grandiflora* makes a beautiful low-growing hedge; good plants can be bought for six dollars a hundred. *Berberis Thunbergii*, or Barberry, makes a fine hedge, on account of its beautiful foliage and scarlet fruit. It is, however, slow-growing.

The owner of a small place should avoid the temptation to scatter flower beds about the lawn. Keep all the planting along the edges of the property and around the house, and leave the lawn unbroken by flower beds.

51

The years when gardening consisted only of beds of Coleus, Geraniums, Verbenas and bedding plants have passed away, like the black walnut period of furniture. And even as the mahogany of our grandfathers is now brought forth from garrets and unused rooms, and antiquity shops and farm-houses are searched for the good old-time furniture, so we are learning to take the old gardens for our models, and the old-fashioned flowers to fill our borders.

The nurseryman of to-day has greatly improved the size and colour of the old varieties of perennials, so that they are far more beautiful than formerly, and offer a much greater choice. By skilful hybridization a hundred or more kinds of Phlox have been developed. In the same way, numerous varieties of Delphiniums, Iris, Peonies, Columbines, Canterbury Bells and Foxgloves have been produced. The old - fashioned annuals also appear in many new forms. In addition to the pink and white " Painted Lady," the pure white and the dark purple Sweet Peas of our mothers' time, we may now cultivate some eighty varieties of this delicate flower. Thus the garden of hardy perennials, annuals and bulbs will give us a continual sequence of flowers in every form and colour from April until November, if properly made and tended.

THE SEED-BED

CHAPTER V

THE SEED-BED

THE possessor of a garden, large or small, should have a seed-bed, where seeds of perennials and some of the annuals can be sown and grown until large enough to be permanently placed. Not only will this bed give great pleasure in enabling one to watch the plants from the time the first tiny leaf appears, but also when laden with blossoms in fullest beauty. The knowledge that you have raised them gives a thrill of pride in the result which no bought plants, however beautiful, can impart. It is not necessary to prepare the seed-bed over a foot in depth, but the soil must be very light and fine, as well as rich. It is best, if possible, to have a portion of the bed somewhat shaded from the sun for a part of the day. If this combination cannot be had in one bed, there should be a second for plants that want less sun. Biennials must, of course, be sown every year, as they bloom but once, then die.

Every year some perennials will disappear, killed by severe winters, by pests of one kind or another, or dying without apparent cause. To keep up the supply, therefore, some of each variety should be raised every year.

Foxgloves and Sweet Williams, if allowed to go to seed, will sow themselves and increase rapidly. The same with Hollyhocks, but, except on the edges of shrubberies and in wild borders, it is better to cut the stalk just before the seed is ready to fall, and save it to sow in the seed-bed.

In my garden, some seventy miles from New York, and where the spring opens ten days later, I sow my seeds,—the perennials about the tenth of April and the annuals from April twentieth to May first. Buy the seeds, if the garden is large, by the ounce or half-ounce; if small, in the seedsman's packets. I always have the seeds of perennials soaked for twenty-four hours before planting, and find that by so doing they are very sure to germinate. Care must be taken, when soaking a number of different kinds at the same time, to place the name of each variety of seed under the glass or bowl containing the same. When ready for planting, pour off the water and mix the wet seeds carefully with very dry earth, in a cigar-box, which is of the right size and easy to handle. Then sow, not too deeply, in rows about a foot apart in the bed, covering very lightly, according to size. One-half inch is enough for the large seeds. The very fine varieties should simply have the earth sprinkled on them. If planted too deep they will never come up. Seeds of annuals do not require soaking.

Pat the earth down firmly with the back of the trowel, sprinkle with a fine sprinkler late every afternoon, and it is not your fault if you do not have hundreds and thousands of young plants to make your own place beau-

tiful and to give to your friends. It is a
keen delight, when a friend says that she has
not raised such and such plants this year, to
run and get your trowel and dig a bunch
of this and that from the rows of sturdy
little plants. It is a pleasure to know that
a bit of your garden has gone to help make
another's beautiful.

One of the greatest pleasures of a garden
is in giving flowers and plants to your
friends. Every October, when arranging the
borders and separating plants, I send away
great boxes of them, some to fortunate
friends with lovely gardens, but without the
same varieties; some to humble cottage gardens, and others to friends who have never
grown a flower, but would like to try. This
year, having made a large new garden, I was
able to give away to friends and neighbors
only about seven hundred plants, not seedlings but large plants and roots. Generally
I can send away far more. Think what a
delight this is!

A request for some plants came to me last autumn from the baggage-master of a railroad station some twenty miles from us, who, by the boxes of shrubs and plants that came to me, inferred that I might have some to spare. I learned that all this man's spare time was spent in his little garden plot, so great was his love of flowers. I know, too, a village expressman (another whom nature intended for a gardener), whose little plot of ground is always a mass of beauty. He has a surprising variety of plants, and every one is a fine specimen of its kind. His *Anemone Japonica alba* are the finest I have ever seen, each one sending up perhaps a dozen slender stalks of the beautiful flowers. I have had great difficulty with this plant and have lost dozens of them. I always drive very slowly by the expressman's garden, burning with envy and wondering how he does it. In fact, it was only last year that I had my first success with these obdurate plants.

They must grow under trees whose branches are sufficiently high to admit the sun half the day. As they bloom in September and October, the tree protects them from the frost, and in winter they should be well covered with stable litter. They are among the few plants to be set out in the spring, for if not well established they are always winter-killed.

It is well not to empty the perennial seed-bed entirely in the autumn, but to leave a few plants of each variety to transplant in the spring, to take the place of those which have not survived the winter. When the bed is empty, in the spring, have a good coating of manure spaded in and proceed again with the sowing.

Biennials, and also most perennials, must be raised every year to keep up the supply.

PLANTING

CHAPTER VI

PLANTING

I CAN NOT impress too strongly upon my readers the importance of ordering their plants and seeds of well-known firms. The best are always the cheapest in the end. Inquiry among friends will generally give the best information as to reliable seedsmen and growers. In ordering shrubs and plants it is important to specify the precise date of delivery, that you may know in advance the day of arrival. The beds or borders should be prepared in advance, so that everything may be set out without delay. Care must be taken that the roots are not exposed to the air and allowed to become dry. It is a good plan, when unpacking a box of plants, to sort them, laying each variety in a pile by itself, covering the roots with the moss and excelsior in which they were packed, and then, if at all dry, to sprinkle thoroughly. Unpacking should, if possible, be done under cover—in the cellar if there be no other place.

Great care must also be taken in setting out plants that ample room be given; as the roots should be well spread out and never doubled up. Do not be afraid of having the hole too big; see that the earth is finely pulverized and well packed about the roots; that the plant is thoroughly soaked, and, if the weather is dry, kept watered for a couple of weeks. If the plants have arrived in good condition and are carefully set out, but few should die. I have never lost a deciduous tree, and frequently, in setting out a hundred shrubs at one time, all have lived.

Wherever there is a fence make a border, wide or narrow according to your space; if wide,—and it may be as much as twelve feet wide,—always make the edge irregular, never straight. Some prefer a hedge at the back of the border. The best effect and quickest screen is made by planting, against the fence at the back of the border, White Lilacs (not the Persian), Syringas, Deutzias and the beautiful new Altheas. Plant these shrubs three feet apart. In good soil they will send up great canes, and in four years time should be six feet high and shut you in from all prying gaze.

In planting a border, always keep in mind the fact that it should be blooming from May to November. Put in the plants according to height, the tallest, of course, at the back and the lowest in front, filling the front also with spring-flowering bulbs, Daffodils, Tulips and Narcissi, which will blossom and be over before the plants come on. You will thus have the longest succession of bloom. If the border is quite wide—from four to six feet—and perhaps one hundred and fifty feet long, it will hold a surprising number of plants.

Certain plants, in a long border with a

background of shrubs, look best in rows, in spite of all that has been written against it: For instance, Hollyhocks, a long row of plants three deep, broken every ten feet or so by a clump of a dozen, and in front of these a single row of Rudbeckias, broken with clumps of six or so, and the rest of the border planted in masses, more or less according to space, of Phloxes, Larkspur, Lilies, Columbines, Sweet Williams, with every now and then a good clump of Chrysanthemums to blossom when all other flowers are gone.

In filling a border along a rather short path, the plants should always be set in clumps of from six to twelve of a kind. If the border is narrow and has no shrubs or hedge back of it, the effect will be better if the plants do not exceed three feet in height. Omit from such a border Hollyhocks, Rudbeckias, Sunflowers and Cosmos. Sweet Williams, Columbines, Sweet Alyssum, Candytuft, Nasturtiums and *Phlox Drummondii* can all be grown as edging for borders.

I have a border, two and a half feet wide and three hundred and fifty feet long, that is a mass of bloom from the middle of May until the last of September.

It may give the reader a suggestion to know its contents. Everything is in rows, the only border in my garden where the planting is done in this way. Along the edge is *Narcissus Poeticus;* back of *Narcissus Poeticus* a row of Sweet Williams, pink, white and very dark red; back of the Sweet Williams, Foxgloves; back of the Foxgloves, Peonies and *Hydrangea grandiflora* planted alternately; and back of these, a row of Hollyhocks. About two feet behind this border, a row of Rudbeckia (Golden Glow) grows like a tall hedge.

When *Narcissus Poeticus* has finished blooming, the Peonies come on. Before the last Peony has lost its petals, the Sweet Williams (quite two feet high) are in blossom, and the Foxgloves (from three to four feet high) begin to bloom, and last for a

69

month. While these flowers are still lovely,
the tall Hollyhocks begin to flower, each
plant sending up from three to five stalks.
Then, by the time the Hollyhock stalks are
cut down, the Hydrangeas, which are trimmed
back very severely every autumn, are a mass
of white. Meanwhile the Rudbeckias, for
quite six weeks, form a yellow background.
The illustrations show this row of flowers
while the Narcissi, Peonies, Foxgloves, and
Hydrangeas are successively in blossom.

Early in June, I transplant into perennial borders, wherever a spot can be found,
clumps of Asters, Cosmos and other late
annuals, which are beautiful in September
and October when most flowers have ceased
to bloom.

From September twentieth to October
fifteenth is a busy time in the garden. New
beds and borders should be made then. The
plants in all borders four years old should
be lifted, and the beds or borders spaded
deeply with plenty of manure, the plants

70

reset, and the young perennials transplanted from the seed-bed into their final places. All perennial plants whose roots are sufficiently large, should now be divided and reset. This fall planting and transplanting should be done at about the time mentioned, for the shrubs and plants must become well rooted before the ground freezes, or they will rarely survive the winter. No matter how rich a bed or border may be, I always have the hole to receive the plant made larger than is necessary, and put a spadeful of manure in the bottom. In transplanting, my man always has a wheelbarrow of this at his side to work from.

If there are bare places in lawns or grass paths, sow grass seed about the twentieth of September, then roll, and the grass will be well rooted before cold weather.

It must be borne in mind that everything possible should be done in the fall. Perennials start early in the spring, and it is a pity, when they are once started, to disturb

71

them. When the frost has finally killed everything, all the dead tops should be cut off at the ground, the dead annuals pulled up, the borders made clean and neat, and, about the last of November, covered with a good layer of stable litter, leaves or straw. I have always found the plants start earlier and do better for this slight protection.

Whenever I tell my inquiring friends of the proper preparation of beds, and the spring top-dressing, and winter covering with manure, there is generally an exclamation of alarm at the quantity used. But much is required to make the garden grow. I call upon the farm for manure when the stable supply is insufficient, and both my farmer-husband and his manager at times look askance. But how can I live unless my garden has what it needs! The farmer-husband looks upon my gardening as a mild species of insanity, and cannot understand why a *little* garden with a few plants is not enough for any woman. By dint of much showing and explanation through many years, he has acquired a floricultural knowledge which enables him to tell a Rose, Lily, Sunflower and Phlox, and of this knowledge he is proud.

All manure should be drawn out into the garden when the ground is still frozen, in March or earlier, and placed in convenient piles, so that the ground may not be cut up, when soft, by the wagon wheels; and also to facilitate work when the first spring days come, and there are a hundred things to be done. If possible, have a spadeful of well-rotted stable manure stirred into the ground around each shrub and vine in early spring. The result will amply repay you. Save all wood-ashes carefully, under cover, for the garden, and scatter them on the beds and on the grass. Get well-ground fresh bone-meal, and let all plants have only a handful in the spring, and the reward in bloom is great. To have good results from the hardy Chrysanthemums the soil cannot be too rich, and I generally "give them something to eat," as a boy who helps in the garden calls it, about the fifteenth of June and the fifteenth of August.

Care must be taken, in using bone-meal, not to put on too much, and to keep it away from contact with the rootlets.

ANNUALS

CHAPTER VII

THERE are so many annuals that I will write only about the few which are easiest to grow and are most desirable. For me a flower must have merits for decorating the house as well as for making the garden beautiful.

The other day I found an English book on flowers, and at once sat down to read it, expecting enjoyment and profit from every page; but at the end of a few minutes I came upon the following paragraph:

> "Particularly to most women one of the chief uses or functions of a garden is to provide flowers to be cut for the decoration of rooms. But I hold that a flower cut from its plant and placed in a vase is as a scalp on the walls of a wigwam."

And I read no further in that book.

I grow flowers to gather them, both for the house and to give away. We keep about sixty vases full in the house from late May until October, and never allow more than two colours in the same room. I have a yellow room, where only yellow and white flowers, or white and blue, are permitted; a pink room, for white and pink or pink and crimson flowers; and a hall, whose dominant tone is a rich red, where the flowers are red and white.

Some of the annuals, like Mignonette and Poppies, must be sown where they are to grow. Mignonette does best in cool, rather moist soil.

Poppies, and oh! have plenty of them and all kinds. Get the Shirley Poppies, the Giant Double, the fringed kind, and the California with their sunny petals. Sow in great numbers wherever they are wanted, here and there in the borders wherever there is space. If there is no other place, sow them in rows in the vegetable garden.

ANNUALS

They are splendid in the house, but, alas! fall too quickly.

The Shirley Poppies are almost like fairy flowers, they are so delicate and beautiful. They are the first of the annual Poppies to bloom. Then comes the variety which grows wild in France and Germany,—scarlet, with black blotches at the base of the petals. Last to bloom are the tall, fringed double and single Poppies,—white, pink and scarlet, growing on strong stems three feet high. Poppies must be sown thinly and the earth only sprinkled over the seeds. Sow as early in the spring as the ground can be worked, and thin out to six inches apart when the plants are well up.

Nasturtiums, too, should be planted where they are to grow, also Sweet Alyssum and Candytuft. All of these make good edgings for borders. If not allowed to go to seed they will bloom all summer.

Sunflowers, the Dwarf Double, and the tall Giant Sunflowers, are fine in backgrounds and against fences.

THE FOLLOWING ANNUALS SHOULD BE SOWN IN THE SEED-BED
ABOUT APRIL TWENTIETH TO MAY FIRST

Antirrhinum, or *Snapdragon*, growing
eighteen inches high. If sown in early May
they will bloom from August until late
autumn. The same is true of the German
Ten-weeks Stocks, which have a long period
of bloom. The white ones are most lovely.

Asters, all varieties; sow a quantity.
They are not only beautiful, but they give
an abundance of blossoms in late September and early October, when flowers are beginning to be scarce. I prefer the Giant,
Comet, Ostrich Plume and the late-flowering
branching kind. Of these last, "Purity"
(snow-white) and "Daybreak" (shell-pink)
are the best, often bearing thirty flowers on
a plant and lasting, in water, five days. A
small quantity of wood-ashes stirred into
the soil of the Aster bed is a fine fertilizer and destroys insects that attack the
roots. Transplant in June to wherever they
are to blossom.

I have lately learned, that the only way to destroy the black beetle which appears upon the Asters and eats the flowers, is to have them picked off morning and evening and thrown into a pan containing kerosene oil, which kills them.

Cosmos. The early-summer flowering variety of Cosmos will begin to bloom in July, and, if not allowed to go to seed, will be a mass of flowers until killed by frost. In favorable soil Cosmos grows luxuriantly, and resembles a small tree six or eight feet high. This plant should be staked, or it is likely to be blown down. It is very effective when transplanted to the borders, blooming gayly when there is not much else. The pink and crimson varieties are beautiful, but do not compare with the white.

Calendula, growing about a foot high in every shade of yellow from deep orange to pale ivory, is one of the best and most constant blooming of the yellow flowers.

Centaurea, or *Cornflower.* These come

81

in many colours, but I grow only the tall,
ragged, blue variety. If not permitted to
go to seed, they will bloom plentifully for
several months. On the dinner-table with
blue and white china, and in June combined
with Syringa, they make a beautiful and
unusual decoration.

Marigold, both the double African and the
double French. These flowers always give
me a pricking of the conscience, for during the summer, when there are plenty of
others, I give them the "go by," but in
October turn to them with shame and thank-
fulness.

Phlox Drummondii grows about six or
eight inches high, and comes in many colours.
It makes beautiful borders, particularly the
white, pink and dark red.

Plumed Celosia, or *Cockscomb*. The new
varieties are very effective.

Zinnias. Lately I have grown only two
varieties, a vivid scarlet and a salmon-pink.
They are not only lovely when growing, but

82

make a beautiful house decoration, as the stems are long and stiff.

Sweet Peas, which no garden can do without. Several books say, plant in autumn, very late. I have twice sown two pounds at this time, carefully following the directions, and not one single Pea came up the following spring. Sweet Peas should be sown in the spring the moment the frost comes out of the ground, so that they may become deeply rooted before dry weather. Make a trench about a foot deep and a foot wide. Have a good layer of manure in the bottom of the trench, over which put a couple of inches of earth, and over this earth put a good layer of wood-ashes, again a sprinkling of earth. Then sow the Peas, and cover them with a couple of inches of earth. As they grow, fill in the trench, and keep on hilling up the plants until the roots are very deep. It is well to mulch them with the clippings of lawn grass. In this way the plants are kept from drying up, and will bloom until October.

Sweet Peas flourish best on a trellis of galvanized wire netting. It should be a permanent trellis, made of cedar posts set three feet deep, so as to be below the frost line and four feet high. To this attach the wire netting. A trench should be made on either side of the netting, so that a double row of Peas may be sown. The quantity sown depends on the length of the trellis; three pounds will sow a double row one hundred and twenty-five feet long. I always sow the different colours separately. It simplifies the task of arranging them, if they can be gathered separately. A bowl of white Sweet Peas and Maidenhair Fern is indeed a "thing of beauty."

Pansies, every one loves them. They are annuals, but do best if treated as biennials. The most practical hint that I was able to get from "Elizabeth's German Garden" was where she spoke of carpeting her Rose beds with Pansies. This instantly appealed to me, as I greatly dislike to see the earth in the beds and borders, and in Rose beds it always is to be seen. So I bought an ounce each of white and yellow Pansy seed, sowed it about the tenth of July in the partly shaded end of the seed-bed, and by October first had splendid great plants. I did not allow these to blossom, but picked off the buds, and, after the Rose beds had been given a plentiful top-dressing of manure carefully stirred in with a large trowel, I transplanted my Pansy plants. Of course, they had to be covered over with the Roses the last of November, and often during the winter I wondered whether the dears would be smothered. On the twenty-eighth of March the beds were uncovered, and, imagine it! there were Pansies in bloom. From April tenth until late in August these beds were simply a carpet of white and yellow. I never saw anything like it. It was probably due to the rich soil, perhaps also to the free water-

ing necessary for the Roses. Then, in order
that no Pansies should go to seed, my own
maid, who is very fond of flowers, undertook
each morning to cut off all that were beginning to wither. This required from one
to two hours, but certainly prolonged the
bloom, and I could never have spared a
man so long for just the Pansies. Sow
Pansy seed in the seed-bed about the tenth
of July, and transplant late in October.

These are some of the more important
annuals which no garden should be without.
All of them are easy to raise, and blossom
abundantly. I do not speak of the many
others, but advise trying new flowers every
year.

The first week in June is the time to
transplant all annuals. Do it, if possible,
directly after a rain, always late in the
afternoon, and, of course, water well after
transplanting. I have a method of my own
for the transplanting of seedlings, and by

following it the tiny plants never wither or are set back, and in fact do not seem to know that they have been moved. Take a tin box, such as biscuits come in, half fill it with water, then lift into it from the seed-bed about one hundred seedlings at a time. With a sharp-pointed stick make holes in the bed where the little plants are to go, and then put them in. Soak the ground thoroughly after each patch is finished. In this way the tiny rootlets never become dry.

All the beds and borders can be kept free from weeds and in good condition if gone over with a trowel every five days, or once a week, the earth stirred thoroughly, and any weeds that may have grown taken out. It is particularly necessary, for a few weeks in the spring, to keep well ahead of the weeds. I always think of my sins when I weed. They grow apace in the same way and are harder still to get rid of. It seems a pity sometimes not to nurture a pet one,

87

just as it does to destroy a beautiful plant of Wild Mustard, or of Queen Anne's Lace.

Asters, all colours; one to two feet; August to October.

Alyssum, white, dwarf for borders; six inches; blooms all summer if not allowed to go to seed.

Balsam, Camellia-flowered, pale pink, dark red, white; two to three feet; July and August.

Calendula (Pot Marigold), all shades of yellow; mid-July until killed by frost.

Calliopsis (Coreopsis), yellow with red or brown center; two feet; mid-July, until killed by frost.

Candytuft, red, white, purple, Empress variety white the best, fine for edging; six inches; blooms continually if not allowed to go to seed.

Centaurea (Cornflower), all shades of blue; three feet; blooms three months if kept cut.

88

Cockscomb, crimson and scarlet; two to three feet; August and September.

Cosmos, white, pink, crimson; three to five feet; from the fifteenth of July until killed by frost.

Eschscholtzia, yellow Poppies; one foot; blooms all summer.

Godetia, pink, crimson, white; one foot; blooms all summer.

Marigold, all shades of yellow; one to two and one-half feet; mid-July until killed by frost.

Mignonette, average height one foot; blooms all summer if kept from seeding.

Nasturtiums, all shades of yellow and red; dwarf, nine inches; climbing, five feet; bloom all summer until killed by frost.

Pansy, many colours; six inches; from early spring until November, if kept well cut.

Petunia, double giant-flowered the only kind to raise; white, crimson and pink; one and one-half feet; bloom all summer.

Phlox Drummondii, many colours; one

foot; blooms July, August and September if not allowed to seed.

Poppy, all shades of pink and red, also white; one to three feet. If several varieties are planted can be had in bloom from three to four weeks; end of June and July.

Snapdragon, scarlet and white, white and yellow, pure white; one and one-half feet; July and August.

Stocks (German Ten-Weeks), white, pink, red, purple; one and one-half feet; middle of July until middle of September.

Sunflower, yellow, dwarf and tall varieties, single and double; three to six feet; all summer.

Sweet Peas, all colours; three feet; grown on bush or trellis; end of June until October if kept well cut and moist.

Sweet Sultan, purple, white, yellow; one and one-half feet; June, July and August.

Zinnia, many colours; one and one-half to two feet; July, August and September.

90

PERENNIALS

CHAPTER VIII

SOME of the perennials to be sown yearly in the seed-bed from about April first to tenth, are the following:

Columbines of all varieties, yellow, white, shading from pink to red and from pale blue to darkest purple.

Of Columbines every garden should have plenty. Blooming about May twentieth for three weeks, they are a perfect delight. They are very hardy, germinate readily in the seed-bed, are easy to transplant and need but little care. I have never been able to get them much over three feet in height, but then I have often a dozen stalks of bloom on a single plant, which is very satisfactory. The first dozen plants were sent to me by a friend from his garden on Long

Island; now I have hundreds of them,—single and double, white, yellow, all shades of red and pink, pale blue, and a blue one with a white center almost like an Orchid; many shades of purple, also purple and white.

Hollyhocks, single and double, of all colours. In order to get the desired colour effect with these, keep each variety separate.

No one can have too many Hollyhocks. Plant them at the back of the borders among the shrubbery, along fences, and in great clumps in any odd corner, or around buildings; they are never amiss, and always beautiful. I find that a Hollyhock cannot be counted upon to bloom more than three years. First-year stalks are about four feet high; afterwards, if in good soil, they will be from six to eight feet. There were hundreds of this size in my garden last summer, each plant with from three to five towering stalks of bloom. As soon as they have gone to seed, I save what seed I want and the stalks are then cut down and burned. By sowing the seeds as soon as thoroughly ripe and dry, plants can be raised which will be large enough to transplant in October, and will bloom the next year. These young plants should be given a slight covering the first winter, that they may not be winter-killed.

When in a border, the Hollyhock, which will flourish in any soil, grows to such an extent that Lilies or Phloxes, or anything else near by, are likely to be crowded out, unless care is taken to cut off the lower leaves, which become enormous. I have this done usually three times before they bloom, beginning early in May, and great wheelbarrow-loads of leaves are taken away at each cutting.

Sweet Williams, red, white and pink. These will grow from eighteen inches to two feet. The stems are straight and stiff, and the trusses of bloom about five inches across, with individual flowers as large as a nickel; they keep well in water and make a beautiful edging for a border, or give great effect when planted in masses. They bloom for

95

three weeks or more, and make fine decorations for church or house.

Platycodon Mariesi, beautiful blue; they resemble Canterbury Bells, and, as they blossom after the Canterbury Bells, are valuable in continuing the period of blue flowers, with the advantage of being perennials.

Delphiniums, perennial Larkspurs, all varieties. These seeds I have found more difficult to make germinate than any others, so I do not rely upon what I raise, but purchase many plants. My best results have come from saving the seeds from the first crop of blossoms, drying thoroughly, and then sowing at once. I have found these seeds more sure to germinate than those bought in early spring. Perhaps nature intends them to be sown in this way, instead of nine months later.

One can never say enough in praise of Delphiniums. Three-year-old plants will send up eight to ten beautiful great spikes of the richest blue, four feet high. The moment a blossom withers, cut the stalk

96

down to the ground; another will immediately spring up. I had four crops of blossoms from some of my Delphiniums last summer, so that, from the end of June until the middle of October, there were always some of them in blossom. Some varieties of tall English Delphiniums are very beautiful. Among them is one, Cœlestinum, of the loveliest shade of light blue, with very large, double individual flowers. As I have said before, the Delphinium blossoms at the same time as *Lilium candidum*, and should be planted near by. Great bunches of these two flowers, in tall vases, are lovely as well as unusual.

There is a horrid small white worm which attacks the roots of the Delphinium, ·and gives no sign until you see the plant dying. I have found that keeping the soil around the plant well covered with coal ashes is a preventive. Delphiniums are hardy and long-lived (unless the worm gets them), and, once planted, they live a dozen years.

Coreopsis (Grandiflora). Every one knows the Coreopsis, which, by continual cutting, will give abundant bloom for three months. The variety with velvety maroon centers is particularly fine.

Hibiscus is very easy to raise, and should be planted among and along the edge of shrubbery. The plants are quite hardy, grow four feet high, and masses of them in pink or white are fine. They bloom in August and September.

Rockets, white and purple. These increase tremendously from self-sowing, so be careful or they will suffocate all that grows near them. I have many plants, all of which have come from a single one that a colored woman gave me a few years ago. She is a nice comfortable old "mammy," black as the ace of spades, with a great love for flowers and a nice patch of them. We have exchanged plants several times. Some of the nicest things I have in my garden came to me in this way, and it is great fun.

98

PERENNIALS

Whenever, in driving about, I see a particularly fine plant in a dooryard, I make friends with its owner, and later suggest that if she (it is usually "she") will give me a small root of this or that, I will bring her some plants or bulbs from my garden, of a kind which she has not. So we are both equally benefited. In this way I was once given a plant of *Valerian*, which has a tall, beautiful white flower with a most delicious odour like vanilla. It blooms for three weeks in late May and early June. From this one plant there are now in the garden a number of large clumps several feet in diameter, and I have given away certainly fifty roots. Valerian is a small white flower in good-sized clusters on long stems, seen now-a-days only in old-fashioned gardens. I am told it cannot be bought of horticulturists.

One must have *Chrysanthemums*, but where the thermometer falls below zero there are not many to be bought, other than the pompon varieties, that will blossom in the garden

before being killed by frost, or that will
survive the winter. Year after year I have
bought dozens of the so-called "September-
flowering Chrysanthemums," and have only
succeeded in making them blossom by the
middle of October, by planting them on the
south side of a building, in richest soil, giving abundance of water, and covering on all
cold nights. But I have beautiful plants of
perfectly hardy, good-sized blossoms of yellow, white, pink and red, the roots of which
have come from the gardens of my farmer
friends. I have never been able to buy this
old-fashioned hardy kind. In the spring, as
soon as the plants begin to sprout, divide
them, setting out three or four sprouts together. In this way the stock will increase
wonderfully.

Chrysanthemums require very rich soil,
must have sun, and do best against a building or a wall. About the first of July and
the first of September have a couple of
trowelfuls of manure carefully dug in about

the roots of each plant. Buds should not be allowed to form until September, and the new shoots should be pinched back until then, to make the plants strong and bushy. I do not envy any one who has only the great, solemn, stiff flowers of the prize-show variety. An armful of the hardy garden ones, with their delicious odour, is worth a green-house full of the unnatural things which are the professional gardener's pride. When you can keep twenty or more vases filled from your own garden with these last blossoms of the year, in all their lovely colours, and not miss one of them from the plants, you will agree with me that they are the only kind to raise.

Perennials, sown in rows in the seed-bed in April, will be nice little plants by July, when they should be lifted and transplanted some six inches apart. The portion of the seed-bed where the annuals were raised can be used now for the purpose. This is particularly necessary for Larkspur, Columbines,

Monkshood, Platycodon, Coreopsis, Hibiscus and Pinks. If, when transplanting, each plant is set with a trowelful of manure, the result will be plants twice as large by the first of October, when they can be again transplanted to their permanent places.

Oriental Poppies and *Pinks* should also be sown in the perennial seed-bed.

Oriental Poppies, with great blossoms as large as a tea plate borne on strong stems, make a grand show about the end of May and beginning of June.

Pinks, too, should be in every garden, if only for their delicious, spicy odor. The Chinensis, or China Pinks, are the best.

Sweet Williams and Oriental Poppies need not be moved from the time they are sown until finally transplanted in the autumn.

Yucca filamentosa, the hardy native of Mexico, sends up, about the tenth of July, great stalks six to eight feet high, bearing masses of white flowers. The individual blossoms are of creamy waxy texture and as beautiful as an orchid. A single stalk of Yucca, in a tall vase, will last nearly a week, and is as unusual as it is beautiful for house decoration. Yuccas are perfectly hardy, need no protection in winter, no fertilizer, no water in dry weather. In my garden, at least, they have not been attacked by insects and have grown placidly on, needing absolutely no care but to have the stalks cut down when they have finished blossoming. They are most effective when grown in clumps, but look very well along a fence with Hollyhocks at the back. The plants are so inexpensive that I have bought mine, but see no reason why they cannot be raised from seed. Small plants form near the parent stem, and these can be separated and transplanted. A late spring frost will sometimes nip the flower stalk that has just started, and there will be no bloom that year. To avoid such a disaster, whenever, in late spring, a frosty night is suspected, cover the plants with a piece of burlap.

103

Tritomas (Red-hot Poker Plant) bloom in September and October, and should always be planted in masses, and in full sun. They must be well covered with leaves or stable litter late in November, or they will be winter-killed. They increase rapidly.

Gaillardias bloom all summer, and keep fresh in water for days. The plants are covered with long-stemmed, yellow flowers with dark crimson centers, and should also be protected in winter.

Veronica longifolia, a most beautiful dark blue flower, which grows in long spikes. Veronica remains in bloom during the month of August, and is one of the most showy flowers in the garden at that time.

Iris, Japanese and German, do well when naturalized in the grass. These plants increase so, that every four years they can be separated. Beginning with the German Iris, flowering the end of May, they can be had in bloom until the Japanese Iris finishes blossoming the middle of July. No Orchids are more beautiful than the Japanese Iris. A couple of weeks before and during the period of bloom they must be kept very moist.

Both the German and the Japanese Iris are perfectly hardy and increase rapidly. The English Iris, of which the white variety, known as Mont Blanc, is the most beautiful, and the Spanish Iris, in all its varieties, are not hardy. But with careful winter covering, about equal to that given to the ever-blooming Roses, they will generally survive, and are well worth the trouble. The roots of all varieties of Iris are very long, and care must be taken to give them plenty of room and to plant deep.

Peonies. For beauty and usefulness Peonies rank with Phloxes. Large plants will frequently bear twenty great blossoms. By raising both early and late varieties, their period of bloom can be continued for a month. The old, dark crimson variety is the first to bloom; the old-fashioned double pink and double white are beautiful enough to satisfy any one, but the new varieties give immense choice as to colour and form.

The Japanese Tree Peonies do not die to the ground every year, like the herbaceous kinds, but form woody branches and grow like a small shrub. The blossoms of these Tree Peonies are truly wonderful; the only care needed is a little fertilizer in the autumn and a slight winter covering. They are best grown in front of the shrubbery. They blossom before the herbaceous varieties. The herbaceous Peonies can be grown in large beds by themselves, in borders with other plants, or as single specimens in the grass or among the shrubs.

Peonies start so early in the spring that they should be manured in the fall, or there is danger of breaking the tender shoots.

Phlox. There is no flower in the garden more beautiful, more easily cultivated, or giving so much bloom as the Phlox. I could certainly never have a garden without it.

In mine there must be a couple of thousand. I have a great mass, of probably two hundred herbaceous Phloxes, growing together in one corner of my garden, the very tall varieties over four feet high. About the fifteenth of July, every year, this corner is a superb sight. Most of these plants are over fifteen years old. They have been kept fine by heaviest top-dressing every year, and by lifting all the plants every three years and digging in quantities of manure, and also by separating each plant into three, by cutting the roots with a spade, or pulling apart with the fingers.

The newer varieties of Phlox come in the most beautiful colours,—dark crimson, fiery scarlet, many shades of pink, pink striped with white, and pink with a white eye; all shades of lilac, lilac with white and purple, the beautiful pure white, and the white with the scarlet eye. Of all the varieties, my favorites are the snowy white, and the salmon-pink with the dark red eye. Buy fifty large field-grown plants; at the end of three years separate them, and you have a hundred and fifty. They present a picture of progression much surer than the tale of the eggs that were to do so much.

Many of the individual blossoms of my Phloxes are larger than a fifty-cent piece; a number of them larger by measurement than a silver dollar, and the heads also are very large. Always erect, neat and smiling, never needing to be staked (such a task in a large garden), when once grown they must always be dear to a gardener's heart. By breaking off the heads of Phlox immediately after blooming, a second crop of flowers will appear in about three weeks. The heads will not be so large as the first, but they will amply repay the slight trouble.

Every owner of a garden has certain favorites; it really cannot be helped, although the knowledge that it is so makes it seem almost as unfair as for a mother to have a favorite child.

PERENNIALS

A real lover of flowers finds it difficult to cast away a plant that has bloomed its best, even though the blossom is unsatisfactory. In my garden there are, at present, some plants that I am longing to dig up and burn. There are two climbing Roses that came by mistake in a large order and were set out. They have thriven as no others, cover a very large space on a trellis, and in June bear thousands of a most hideous, small, purplish crimson Rose. The other plant is *Scabiosia Caucasica*. Beware of the same. The description of it in a catalogue caused me to feel that without it the garden was nothing. A dozen were ordered and set out in a border, in two clumps. They grew and waxed strong, and fairly clambered over everything within several feet of them, seeming to be like gigantic thistles. Finally in August, on stems two feet long, the eagerly looked-for blossoms appeared. These were described in the catalogue as "a large head of pale blue flowers." But, to my despair, it developed a round green ball about three inches in circumference, with white thistle-like petals. And yet the plants had surpassed themselves. It seems a poor reward to turn them out to die.

Lychnis (London Pride). I cannot now recall any perennial except the Cardinal Flower, which has blossoms of so brilliant a scarlet as Lychnis, or London Pride, growing tall and erect, with its bright colour. It is most effective when grown in large clumps.

Monkshood (*Aconitum Napellus*) grows four feet high, and has a beautiful blossom of rich blue growing in quite large clusters. The name must come from the resemblance each individual blossom bears to the capuchin of a monk. These plants should be grown under tall trees, for they cannot stand too strong sun, and will blossom very late in the autumn if protected by the trees from frost. I gathered them last year in November.

110

Phloxes, Rudbeckias, Monkshood, Valerian,
Lychnis, Tritomas, Iris, Peonies and Veronica are best raised, not from seed, but by
buying the plants, and then after a time,
as I have said before, dividing them. For
instance, take a fine large plant of Phlox
of some choice variety, divide all the roots
and set out each one separately. From one
plant you may, in two years' time, get twenty
splendid ones, and the same with the other
varieties I have mentioned.

Rudbeckias, of the Golden Glow variety,
grow from six to eight feet high, and must
be staked, or when heavy with blossoms
they will blow down or be beaten down by
the rain. Each plant will bear quantities of
long-stemmed double yellow blossoms, which
resemble a double Dahlia. These will keep
nearly a week in water. When the plant
has finished blossoming, cut down the tops,
and in October there will be a second crop
of blossoms just above the ground.

The Golden Glow should be divided every

other year, and in this way it is even more remunerative than the Phlox. I started with fifty plants, and think it will soon be possible to have a farm of them.

LIST OF HARDY PERENNIALS, WITH HEIGHT, COLOUR AND TIME AND PERIOD OF BLOOMING, ARRANGED ALPHABETICALLY.

Aquilegia, or Columbine, all colours; one to two and one-half feet; tenth of May to first week in June.

Chrysanthemums, all colours but blue; three feet; end of September until very cold weather.

Delphiniums, all shades of blue; three to four feet; July; later crops after cutting down.

Dianthus barbatus (Sweet William), red, pink, white; one to two feet; June.

Dicentra spectabilis (Bleeding Heart), red and white; one to two feet; May.

Gaillardia, yellow, red center; two feet; July, August and September until killed by frost.

112

Helianthus multiflorus plenus, hardy double Sunflower; yellow; four to five feet; all summer.

Hibiscus, pink, white; four to five feet; August and September.

Hollyhocks, all colours but blue; single, double, four to eight feet; tenth of July to middle of August; two to five stalks on a plant.

Hyacinthus candicans, white; four feet; last three weeks of August.

Iris Germanica, all colours; two to three feet; end of May to first of June.

Lychnis (London Pride), scarlet; two and one-half feet; July.

Oriental Poppy, scarlet, also pink; three feet; end of May and first of June.

Peonies, all colours but blue; two to two and one-half feet; end of May, for three weeks.

Pentstemon, many colours; three feet; August and September.

Phlox, all colours; two to four feet; early

July until killed by frost, if the heads are cut as soon as finished flowering.

Platycodon Mariesi, blue; one and one-half feet; August.

Rocket (*Hesperis Matronalis*), white and purple; two feet; May.

Rudbeckia (Golden Glow), yellow; five to eight feet; middle of July to September first; second crop in October.

Tritoma (Red-hot Poker Plant), orange-scarlet; three to four feet; September and October until killed by frost.

Valerian, white; three feet; May and June.

Veronica longifolia, blue; two feet; August.

Yucca filamentosa, white; three to five feet; second and third weeks in July.

BIENNIALS AND A FEW BEDDING-OUT PLANTS

CHAPTER IX

BIENNIALS AND A FEW BEDDING-OUT PLANTS

THERE are but few hardy biennials. The important ones, which no garden should be without, are: *Digitalis* (Foxgloves) and *Campanula medium*, (Canterbury Bells.)

Foxgloves and Canterbury Bells bloom in June and July for more than a month, and give a touch of glory to any garden.

Catalogues and many gardening books say that the seeds should be sown in early autumn, and the plants will bloom the following year. It is true that they will bloom when sown in the autumn, but unless kept over the winter in a cold-frame the plants will send up stalks, only about a foot in height.

Sow the seeds of Foxgloves and Canterbury Bells in the shady part of the seed-

117

bed in early April. Keep the young plants moist. About the fifteenth of July, if there are a large number of plants and there be no other place, they should be transplanted to the vegetable garden, where they can follow early crops of peas or lettuce. Have the ground spaded finely, and make shallow trenches, perhaps six inches deep, in which put a good layer of manure and cover this with earth, then set the plants about six inches apart. Keep them well watered when the weather is dry, and the earth thoroughly stirred. By the twentieth of September or the first of October they should be transplanted to the places where they are to bloom the following year. The plants should then be a foot across, and next June will send up several stalks about three feet high. The Canterbury Bells should be six inches across in the fall, and the next year about two feet high.

Foxgloves seed themselves with great abundance, unless the stalk is cut before the

118

seed ripens. In the spring I have the little plants, seeded in this way from the year before, taken from the borders and transplanted in rows, and find they are larger and stronger than any others.

Foxgloves, white, spotted and pale lilac, are the pride of the garden. Plant them back of the Sweet Williams, in clumps of six or eight, or else with Peonies. They blossom at the same time, and the pinks or reds of Sweet Williams or Peonies, with here and there a mass of white, and the tall, graceful spikes of the Foxgloves rising above them, produce so beautiful an effect that you will simply have to go and look at them many times a day.

Canterbury Bells. Let any one who has been at Oxford in June and July recall the Canterbury Bells in those loveliest of all gardens, New College and St. Johns, and she will not rest until they have a place in her garden. I did not know these flowers before going to Oxford, and after seeing them

119

could not wait to raise them from seed, but bought three dozen plants to look at the first year. The roots that came to me were miserable little things, and, in spite of every care, half of them died. Those which lived and bloomed were very lovely. They begin to blossom with us about the sixth of June, and last four or five weeks. In colour they are white, pink, purple and blue.

Canterbury Bells and Foxgloves are biennials. They are sown one year and grow for a year, then bloom and die. This seems a great deal of trouble for one season's flowers, but their beauty repays the gardener a hundred fold. They require a slight winter protection of leaves or stable litter, but care must be taken that the tops of the plants are not covered.

THE BEDDING-OUT PLANTS

And now a little about the only three bedding-out plants that I grow—Dahlias, Cannas and Gladioli. I should have said four, for there is always a large bed of about four dozen Scarlet Salvia (the Bonfire variety is the best), whose brilliant colour and sturdy growth cannot be spared. They begin to blossom in July. By driving a tall stake in the center, and other stakes around the edge of the bed of Salvia, it can be covered with burlaps or carriage covers when the nights are frosty and preserved in all its beauty until November.

Dahlias can be grown in rows in the vegetable garden, if there be no other place for them. They are decorative and desirable for cutting. Plant two or three tubers in a hill about the third week in April. They should be planted eight inches deep and three feet apart, and kept well staked. The soil should not be too rich, or they will all grow to stalk and leaf, and blossom but little. All the varieties are lovely, the Cactus kind more so, perhaps, than the others. In the autumn, when the tops have been killed by the frost, the tubers must be taken up, dried off carefully, and stored in a cellar that does not freeze.

Gladioli can be planted from April fifteenth to June fifteenth, in beds by themselves or in clumps in the borders, so that the blossoms may be had in succession. Gladioli come in many colours.

Cannas, the beautiful French varieties. These, of course, are most effectively grown in masses, and require full sun. The roots, like those of the Dahlias, increase so that there is almost double the quantity to plant the next spring. It is well to have the Cannas started in boxes in sunny windows, in tool-room or carriage-house, by mid-April. They can be kept through the winter with the Dahlias and Gladioli.

ROSES

CHAPTER X

ROSES

THE Rose asserts her right to the title of the "queen of flowers" through her very exclusiveness. She insists upon being grown apart from other plants; otherwise she sulks and is coy, refusing to yield more than an occasional bloom. I speak from experience, having tried several times to grow Roses in the front of wide borders, where soil and sun and everything except the proximity of other plants was propitious. But they scarcely bloomed at all. Now, the same bushes, planted in rows so that a cultivator may be run between them, flourish satisfactorily. Grow Roses, then, in beds by themselves or in rows.

If one has but half a dozen Roses, let them be grown apart from other plants.

Pansies, however, can be grown in the Rose beds, as I have elsewhere described; Gladioli can also be planted among them without detriment to either. The reason for this is that the roots of these two flowers are not deep and do not interfere with the nourishment of the Roses.

Roses on their own roots should live for years, if given proper treatment. Witness the Rose bushes in gardens, where with but little care they have flourished more than a generation.

Budded stock must be planted very deep. The joint should be at least three inches under ground. Roses grown on their own roots are more expensive than the budded stock, but a far better investment. The budded stock is apt to send up from the parent root suckers or shoots of Sweetbrier, Buckthorn, Flowering Almond, or whatever it may be. These shoots must be carefully cut off. A friend told me that, when new to Rose growing, his bed of budded Roses

126

sent up so many strange shoots that, not knowing what to do, he dug them all up but one. This he kept as a curiosity, and now it is a bush of Flowering Almond six feet in circumference.

Everblooming Roses should be set out in the spring, about the middle of April.

Hybrid Perpetual and Hardy Roses are best set out in autumn, about October tenth. When planting, always cut the plants back to about a foot in height.

All Roses should be lifted every three years, late in October, and plenty of manure, with fresh earth and leaf-mould, mixed with sand if the soil is heavy, dug in.

After five or six years I dig up my Roses about October tenth, cut the tops down to about twelve inches, cut out some of the old wood, cut off the roots considerably, trench the ground anew, and replant. The following year the Roses may not bloom very profusely, but afterwards for four or five years the yield will be great. My physician in the country is a fine gardener, and particularly successful with Roses. We have many delightful talks about gardening. When I told him of my surgical operations upon the Roses he was horrified at such barbarity, and seemed to listen with more or less incredulity. So I asked him if, as a surgeon as well as physician, he approved, on occasion, of lopping off a patient's limbs to prolong his life, why he should not also sanction the same operation in the vegetable kingdom. He was silent.

I shall not say much about Roses, because there is so much to say. They need a book by themselves, and many have already been written. In my garden there are not more than five hundred Roses, including the climbing varieties. They have done very well, and have not been given more care than other plants.

For years I did not grow Roses, fearing they would not be a success. I had read about the beetles and spiders and other

creatures that attack them, and dreaded the
spraying and insect - picking that all the
books said must be done. But, of course,
I finally yielded to the temptation of having the very flower of all flowers, in my
garden, and have found the trouble slight
and the reward great. I have them in beds
in a little formal garden, and in rows in a
picking garden.

The beds and the trenches for the rows
are both made in the usual way, and every
fall, in late October, before the Pansies are
set out as already described, manure is dug
in, and in the early spring, about the tenth
of April, a handful of finely ground fresh
bone-meal is stirred in around each plant
with a trowel. They are sprayed with slug-
shot three times between April tenth and
May fifteenth, when they get a thorough
spraying with kerosene emulsion, and, as a
result, my Roses are not troubled with the
usual pests.

In November the hardy perpetuals are all

cut back to about two feet in height, and
the old wood is thinned out. The everblooming Roses are cut back to a foot in
height. And Roses! well, really, no one
could ask better from a garden. I have not
many varieties, but when I left the country
last fall, the tenth of November, although ice
nearly an inch in thickness had formed, there
were Roses still in bloom in the garden.

The very hardy Roses, which, with a few
exceptions, bloom only in June and early
July, with an occasional flower in the autumn, should be planted together, as they
need but slight covering. In late November
the hardy ones get about a foot of stable
litter over the beds. The everblooming
kinds have six inches of manure, then a
foot of leaves, and then a good covering of
cedar branches over all. But cover late and
uncover early (the very minute the frost is
out of the ground), or your Roses will die.

If asked to name, from my own experience, the best dozen Roses, I should say the

130

following were the most satisfactory: General Jacqueminot, Jubilee, Ulrich Brunner, Madame Plantier, Clothilde Soupert, Kaiserin Augusta Victoria, La France, Mrs. Robert Garrett, Princess Alice de Monaco, Soleil d'Or, Perle des Jardins, and Mrs. John Laing or Baroness Rothschild. Paul Neyron and Prince Camille de Rohan might also be added to the list.

Between Mrs. John Laing and Baroness Rothschild, it is a toss-up. Mrs. John Laing is a healthy, strong Rose, and a most constant bloomer. But none that grows is more beautiful than the Baroness Rothschild. Rather a shy bloomer; still each Rose, on its long, strong stem, surrounded by the very fine foliage that distinguishes this variety, makes a bouquet in itself. Baroness Rothschild is also vigorous, and I have never seen it attacked by the enemies of most Roses.

Climbing Roses have so much use, as well as beauty, in a garden, that my advice is, wherever there is an excuse for having one, plant it there. They do finely on the south side of a house, on arches, summer-houses and trellises. I have a trellis along one side of a grass walk three hundred and fifty feet long. At each post are planted two Roses, a Crimson Rambler and a Wichuraiana. The Wichuraiana blossoms when the Rambler is done. Imagine the beauty of this trellis when the Roses are in bloom! On the other side of this walk there is a border four feet wide, with shrubs at the back, filled, all of the three hundred and fifty feet, with many varieties of perennials, also with Lilies and annuals planted in wherever a foot of space can be found.

All of the Ramblers are good, but none blooms so luxuriantly as the crimson. The Climbing Clothilde Soupert, Baltimore Belle and Climbing Wootton are also fine. Of the Wichuraiana Hybrids, Jersey Beauty and Evergreen Gem are the best. The foliage is lovely, and the perfume of the flowers delicious.

ROSES

The Climbing Roses should be yearly enriched in the spring with manure and bonemeal, and, after two years, some old wood should be cut out every autumn. Many of the Crimson Ramblers and Wichuraiana in my garden made growth last summer of splendid great canes, larger around than one's thumb and from ten to fourteen feet long. Monday was the day for tying and training the Roses, and often it seemed impossible for them to grow so much in a week. It would have been incredible, had we not the actual proof before our eyes.

Red

General Jacqueminot.
Prince Camille de Rohan, (darkest Rose of all).
Jubilee.
Baron Bonstetten.
General Washington.
John Hopper.
Ulrich Brunner.
Victor Verdier.

133

A WOMAN'S HARDY GARDEN

Pink

Mrs. John Laing (constant bloomer).
Anne de Diesbach.
La France (blooms all summer).
Magna Charta.
Mme. Gabriel Luizet.
Baroness Rothschild.
Paul Neyron.

White

Margaret Dickson.
Coquette des Alpes.
White Maman Cochet (blooms continually).
Madame Plantier (blooms continually).
Coquette des Blanches.
Mme. Alfred Carriere.
Marchioness of Londonderry.

Yellow

I know but two hardy yellow Roses:

The Persian Yellow.
Soleil d'Or.

The monthly or everblooming Roses, which need very heavy covering in winter, should be planted together. The following are a few of the best and most constant bloomers:

Kaiserin Augusta Victoria, white.
Bride, white.

ROSES

Clothilde Soupert, white with faint blush center.

Madame Hoste, creamy white.

Perle des Jardins, yellow.

Sunset, yellow.

Mlle. Germaine Trochon, yellow.

American Beauty, rich crimson.

Marion Dingee, deep crimson.

Souvenir de Wootton, crimson.

Bridesmaid, pink.

Hermosa, pink.

Madame de Watteville, pink.

Burbank, pink.

Mrs. Robert Garrett, pink.

Princess Alice de Monaco, petals white, edged with
    blush-pink.

LILIES

CHAPTER XI

LILIES

LILIES, too, should have a book for themselves. My knowledge of them is slight. *Lilium auratum* (Auratum Lily), the grandest of all Lilies, disappears after a few years. If large-sized bulbs are bought there will be the first year from twenty to thirty Lilies on a stalk four feet high, the second year seven to ten, the third year perhaps two or three, but oftener none at all. If you then dig for the bulb, lo! it is gone. The expense, therefore, of these Lilies is great, from their having to be often renewed. Still, do not fail to have them, if possible, for nothing can take their place. They bloom from the middle of July for about a month.

I wrote to an authority on Lilies to ask the cause of this disappearance. He told

139

me that, as soon as planted in this country, a microbe disease attacked them and they gradually disappeared under its ravages. Botanists surely should find a specific, or antidote for this; but perhaps, like some of the most terrible diseases of the human being, it evades all research. Miss Jekyll, in her book on Lilies for English Gardens, in speaking of *Lilium auratum* says:

> "This grand Lily, well planted, and left alone for three years, will probably then be at its best. After this the bulbs will be likely to have increased so much that it will be well to divide them."

This would seem to imply that the Auratums thrive in England. Well, they have climate in England, even if we have weather, and English gardens will always fill American gardeners with despair.

Lilium candidum, which blooms before the other Lilies, is hardy and fragrant and increases rapidly. These Lilies must have full sun and light soil. About every three or four years they can be separated, which should be done as soon as the stalks turn yellow, as the bulb makes an autumn growth. For this reason the Candidums must always be bought and planted by the tenth of September. Other Lilies may be planted in the spring, when the frost leaves the ground, or in October.

Lilium speciosum rubrum thrives and increases in our climate, needs a partly shaded location and, therefore, does well when planted among Rhododendrons. It blooms after the Auratum, the end of August and first two weeks of September.

Lilium speciosum album blooms at the same time as *Lilium rubrum*. It is a beautiful pure white Lily with wax-like curved petals, grows best in full sun, and averages six Lilies on a stalk, although I have often counted more.

Lilium longiflorum blooms early in July. These lilies are very much like the Bermuda Lily, except that they have, as a rule, about

141

four blossoms on a stalk, and are hardy. In my garden they have not increased.

Hansoni, a Japanese Lily, flowering in June; bright yellow in color; perfectly hardy and very desirable.

Lilium Canadense (the Meadow Lily), yellow, red and orange, increases, and is very satisfactory, but likes as moist a situation as possible.

Tigrinum, the old Tiger Lilies, both single and double. These bloom in July, increase rapidly, and by planting, when fully ripened, the little black bulbils which form on the stalk, any number of bulbs can be raised.

Funkia subcordata is the old-fashioned white Day Lily of our grandmothers' gardens. The broad leaves of this plant are almost as handsome as the spikes of bloom. These Lilies flower best when grown in the sun, but then the leaves turn yellow—so give them a partly shaded place.

Funkia cœrulea, with the blue blossom,

is worthy of a place in the garden, though far from being as effective as the white-flowered variety. I also grow the kind with the small white and green variegated leaves for the sake of the foliage, so useful in house decoration.

Funkias are not, botanically speaking, Lilies, but are mentioned in this chapter because popularly known as Day Lilies and on account of the lily-like form of their blossoms.

Lily-of-the-valley should have a place in every garden. Absolutely hardy, requiring no care, it blooms prolifically in early May, fills the air with its fragrance, and is beloved by every one. The German name for this flower, Mai Glöcken (May Bells) is particularly appropriate. I have heard of one woman whose bed of these flowers, four feet by fifty feet, has yielded as many as twenty thousand sprays in one season. The pips can be set out the end of October or the beginning of November. If the bed is quite

143

large, when the Lilies have finished blooming, some can be lifted here and there and transplanted. As the pips increase rapidly, their places will soon be filled. Lilies-of-the-valley do best in a partially shaded place, and require a deep, rich soil, well mixed with leaf-mould.

A Lily bed should be prepared, if the place is damp and drainage not good, by digging out the soil for three feet, and putting a foot of cobblestones in the bottom; then fill up with a mixture of good soil, leaf-mould and sand, and very old, well-rotted manure. In the ordinary garden that is not wet, two feet are enough to dig out the bed, and the cobblestones can be omitted. Lilies should always be set with a handful of sand around the bulb, to prevent any possibility of manure coming in contact with it, as the manure will destroy the bulb.

In my garden there is no special place prepared for the Lilies, but they are grown in all the borders, the *Rubrums* in the shade, the others in the sun, and this year there have been thousands of them. If there are no woods near, where the men can gather leaf-mould, have the rakings of the autumn leaves put in a pile, cover with boards, and occasionally during the spring and summer have them well forked over; the next autumn there will be a quantity of the finest thing for Lilies, Rhododendrons, Ferns, or indeed any kind of plant. This should be mixed in a pile in the proportion of one wheelbarrow of mould, two of good soil, two coal-scuttlefuls of wood ashes, one-half barrow of old manure and two spadefuls of fine bone-meal. There is also nothing better for the Roses than some of this mixture.

All Lilies do better if well mulched with clippings of lawn grass or with very old manure.

The varieties of Lilies mentioned are the easiest grown and the most satisfactory.

Lilies should always be planted in clumps

of the same kind—never less than six, and the number increased according to the size of the garden. Alternate clumps of a dozen each of *Lilium auratum* and *Lilium album* planted in a border just behind Foxgloves and Canterbury Bells will come into bloom when these two biennials have finished, the *Auratum* first, then the *Album*; these four flowers will keep the border gay from early in June until the middle of September.

Lilies should be planted about eight inches deep, and have a covering of litter late in the autumn.

SPRING-FLOWERING BULBS

CHAPTER XII

SPRING-FLOWERING BULBS

BULBS can be planted at any time in the autumn before the ground freezes; the first week in November is as good a time as any. The cost of Tulips, Narcissi and Daffodils is not great. They multiply and need not be disturbed for three or four years.

Snowdrops. The earliest of all flowers to bloom is the Snowdrop. After the long, cold winter, with the melting of the snow and the first suspicion of milder air, these frail beauties send up their graceful bells of white. With what triumph the first one is found and brought to the house, and what a thrill of joy it gives to know that spring will soon be here! Snowdrops can be planted thickly in the borders and also, like Crocuses, in

149

the grass. The foliage of both will die before it is time to mow the lawn.

Crocuses, which should be planted in the grass, will begin to bloom as soon as the Snowdrops pass. The gay little things make the lawn, while still brown, a carpet of bright colors. I heard of a gentleman who planted ten thousand of them in this way, and was rewarded by a most beautiful display at a time when there were no other flowers.

Tulips I plant everywhere in the borders about four inches apart, all kinds, such as single, double, Gesnerianas and Parrot Tulips; but always a quantity of only one kind together. The bed where later the Salvias are put, has three hundred Golden Yellow Tulips. When these have faded, the Salvia plants are set out in the same bed, without disturbing the bulbs. This can be done if the men are careful, and when the Tulip leaves are quite yellow they are cut off (for unless allowed to ripen the bulb does not grow and multiply.) Every three years all Tulips are dug up in the autumn, after the Salvias have died; the bed is then made very rich, and the Tulips reset. There are generally more than enough to refill the bed. The same treatment is pursued in the Canna bed, only here the Tulips are double white.

Tulips will bloom from April twentieth until the last of May, if both the very early as well as the late kinds are planted. The late varieties are the Parrot and Gesneriana, which latter grow two feet high and are very showy.

I have been constantly surprised to find that many good gardeners take up all bulbs when through flowering in the spring, store through the summer and replant in the autumn. This is not only unnecessary, but it is better for the bulbs to remain in the ground as nature intended. Mine have always been so treated and have been successful.

In planting bulbs in newly prepared soil, great care must be taken that they do not come in contact with manure. To prevent this, the man should have a box of sand, in a handful of which each bulb should be set. Spring flowering bulbs should be planted about four inches deep.

Poeticus Narcissus and *Daffodils*, both single and double, do well when naturalized in grass that need not be cut until the foliage of the bulb has died in June. They also make a very good edging for a border along a walk.

The single Van Sion and Emperor Narcissus are excellent varieties. The old-fashioned sweet-scented Jonquil and double Van Sion, or Double Yellow Daffodil, are as satisfactory as any of the numerous kinds named in the catalogues. One early spring, the Double Yellow Daffodils were all in bloom on the tenth of April.

Narcissi and Daffodils live for generations. I know some double yellow Daffodils growing in my great-grandfather's garden, that were planted over seventy years ago. The place was

152

sold and the house burned about thirty years since, and all this time has been entirely neglected. Some one told me that Daffodils and Narcissi still bloomed there bravely in the grass. With a cousin, one lovely day last spring, I took the train out to this old place and there found quantities of the dainty yellow flowers. We had come unprovided with any gardening implements, having nothing of the kind in town, and brought only a basket for the spoils, and a steel table-knife. We quickly found the knife of no avail, so borrowed a sadly broken coal-shovel from a tumble-down sort of a man who stood gazing at us from the door of a tumble-down house. The roots of the Daffodils were very deep, and neither of us could use a spade, so the driver of the ramshackle wagon taken at the station was pressed into service. Handling of shovel or spade was evidently an unknown art to him. The Daffodil roots were nearly a foot deep , but we finally got them, several hundreds of them, all we could

carry. The driver seemed to think us somewhat mad and said "Them's only some kind
of weed," but when I told him the original
bulbs from which all these had come were
planted by my great-grandmother and her
daughter, and that I wanted to carry some
away, to plant in my own garden, he became interested and dug with all his heart.
The bulbs were in solid clumps a foot across
and had to be pulled apart and separated.
They were the old Double Yellow Daffodil
and a very large double white variety, the
edges of the petals faintly tinged with yellow
and delightfully fragrant. My share of the
spoils is now thriving in my garden. By
the process of division every three years,
these Daffodils can be made to yield indefi-
nitely, and perhaps some great-grandchild of
my own may gather their blossoms.

Hyacinths, too, should have a place in
the spring garden. They are more expensive, as a rule, than Tulips, Narcissi and
Daffodils, but, in large or small quantities,

are well worth the money. The single varieties are generally preferred, while, of all kinds, the white and pale blue are the loveliest.

Nothing in the garden gives so much pleasure as the early spring flowers. Perhaps this is because they are the first to bloom. Every one knows how beautiful the first lovely Dandelion seems, gold-starring the new grass. Many bulbs can be had for little money, and I would say to all, plant as many as you can squeeze in. From April fifteenth to May fifteenth I receive in town, twice a week, great boxes of spring flowers from my garden, enough each time to fill sixteen to twenty vases; yet my orders to the men are to cut always so that the flowers cannot be missed from the garden.

SHRUBS

CHAPTER XIII

SHRUBS

OF the hundreds of shrubs, comparatively few survive the severe winter climate of interior New York, or grow very luxuriantly.

Lilacs of all varieties, white and purple, single and double; Deutzias, white and pink; and Syringa, the improved large-flowered variety, are most beautiful. *Spiræa Van Houttei*, sometimes called Bridal Wreath, with its long trails of white blossoms; and *Viburnum plicatum*, or Japanese Snowball, which in late May bears a ball of bloom on every twig and is both healthy and hardy, are also desirable shrubs. The old variety of Snowball is attacked by a blight, the leaves curl up and grow black and the blooms are imperfect. A few years ago I dug up all of mine and burned them.

159

Altheas, or Rose of Sharon,—not by any means the old purplish red variety, but the beautiful new double white and double pale pink kinds, with blossoms coming in August and reminding one of Camellias,—are indispensable. Do not fail to have *Hydrangea paniculata*, with its great heads of white bloom, slowly changing to dull pink, and lasting quite six weeks.

Japanese Barberry, a dwarf shrub, covered in autumn with scarlet berries which remain on the bush all winter, is very ornamental. Many of us remember *Calycanthus floridus*, or the Sweet-scented Shrub of our young days, when the children would tie two or three of the queer brown blossoms in the corner of a handkerchief to regale their less fortunate companions with a sniff of the delicious odor. *Forsythia* and *Laburnum*, or Golden Chain, both have yellow blossoms. Others are, *Weigela Rosea*, the well-known pink-flowering shrub; *Rhus Cotinus*, or Purple Fringe, and *Cydonia Japonica*, or Japanese

160

Quince, deep rose-pink, flowering early in the spring.

These all yield beautiful flowers, beside being hardy and of rapid growth.

All shrubs should be trimmed as soon as they have finished flowering, but only enough to prevent their becoming spindling, with the exception of *Hydrangea grandiflora*, which should be trimmed back, at least three-quarters of the new growth, every year.

It is important, also, to thin out the old wood of most shrubs after five or six years.

Shrubs can be grown from cuttings if one has patience to wait for the result. But as it takes from three to four years' time and considerable care to grow a shrub that would cost but twenty cents, for which price many varieties of shrubs can be bought, few people care to raise them.

On a large place it might be worth while to raise shrubs from cuttings. And where there is plenty of space, a small nursery of them might be kept.

At the end of June take clippings about a foot long, make a shallow trench in good ground and plant them a couple of inches deep. They should be well rooted, in about six weeks. If the weather be dry, after planting them, they must be watered daily. The following spring they should be reset, a foot apart, where they can grow until transplanted to their final resting place. I know a beautiful hedge of *Cydonia Japonica*, or Japanese Quince, that has been grown from cuttings. Privet can easily be grown from cuttings, and I have raised Box from clippings. Fortunately, the season was a wet one, for if allowed to become dry before being well rooted, they would probably have died.

List of Most Satisfactory Shrubs

Altheas, pink or white; blooms in August. Jeanne d'Arc, pure double white, the best. Grows six to eight feet in five years; must be trimmed in October.

Berberis Thunbergii, or Barberry, of slow growth; about three feet high; desirable for its beautiful foliage and scarlet fruit in winter.

Calycanthus floridus, or Sweet - scented Shrub. It yields its brown blossoms the end of May; slow-growing; requires but little trimming; height, five to six feet.

Cydonia Japonica, Japanese Quince, has brilliant red blossoms in early May; grows six to seven feet high.

Deutzia crenata, variety of pale pink, and *Candidissima,* white; of rapid growth, and very high; six to eight feet in five years.

Forsythia blooms in April with masses of yellow flowers; moderate, quick growth; seldom over six feet high.

Hydrangea paniculata grandiflora, the finest of all hardy shrubs. The flowers are great panicles of white. They bloom about the first of August and remain beautiful for six weeks, slowly changing to a soft, dull pink. This shrub is most effective when grown in masses of a dozen or more, although single specimens are very fine. They must be vigorously cut back late every fall, leaving only about six inches of new growth.

Lilac, common purple and common white; also *Marie Legray*, a fine white Lilac, and *Madame Lemoine*, a new double variety bearing very large trusses of flowers. All of these varieties of Lilac grow high and rapidly —frequently eight feet in six years. They require little or no pruning. It is sufficient to cut the blossoms either before or after they go to seed.

Lonicera rosea and *Lonicera albida*, upright Honeysuckles, in shrub form, vigorous, quick-growing, requiring but slight pruning in late autumn. They flower in May, and in midsummer are covered with beautiful berries.

Magnolia conspicua, with large white blossoms, blooms the middle of April; *Soulangeana* has large pink flowers and blossoms

164

the end of April. Magnolias should be pruned when set out, and should be moved only in spring.

Philadelphus syringa, or Mock Orange; *grandiflorus* is the finest. The flowers are pure white, very fragrant and bloom about the middle of June. The shrub grows high, is perfectly hardy and in every way satisfactory. It should be trimmed as soon as it has finished blossoming. Cut back about three-quarters of the new growth; it will then send out side shoots and become continually thicker.

Privet. The common Privet is of very rapid growth and excellent for a screen. It should be trimmed the end of June, but only enough to prevent its becoming scraggly. The California Privet is not so hardy.

Rhus Cotinus, popularly known as Smoke Tree or Purple Fringe, grows as high as a small tree and requires almost no pruning. In midsummer it is covered with fine, mist-like, purple flowers.

Spiræa Van Houttei. This is one of the most satisfactory shrubs; is rather dwarf in habit, growing about five feet high. The end of May it is covered with clusters of white flowers on long, pendulous branches. Trim as soon as it has finished blooming, cutting off about half of the new growth.

Spiræa Anthony Waterer, another Spirea, very dwarf, only about a foot in height, and covered with bright crimson flowers from June to October.

Viburnum plicatum, Japan Snowball, one of the finest shrubs. It grows about six feet high, and is completely covered with its balls of snow in early June. It requires comparatively little trimming.

Weigela.—The two most satisfactory varieties of this shrub are *Candida*, whose blossoms are white, and *Rosea*, with pink flowers. They bloom most freely about the tenth of June, when each shrub becomes a mass of flowers. Care must be taken to cut out the old wood from time to time, and to trim after the shrub has finished blooming.

Of evergreen shrubs, *Kalmia latifolia,* or Mountain Laurel, is most satisfactory, growing three to four feet high. It is covered in early June with large clusters of pale pink and white flowers.

Rhododendron maximum, the large-leaved hardy American variety. Under cultivation this shrub seldom grows more than six feet high ; in the woods it is found much larger.

Japanese Holly, a dense-growing shrub about four feet high, with deep glossy green foliage.

Tree Box, generally trimmed in standard or pyramidal form and very slow-growing.

Ampelopsis quinquefolia, Virginia Creeper.
Ampelopsis Veitchi, Boston Ivy.
Aristolochia Sipho, Dutchman's Pipe.
Bignonia radicans, Trumpet Creeper.

167

Clematis paniculata, clusters of fine white flowers.

Clematis Henryi, large white flowers.

Clematis Jackmani, large purple flowers.

English Ivy.

Honeysuckle, Hall's Japan, Golden Japan.

Hops.

Vitis Coignetiæ, Japanese ornamental grape-vine; rapid grower.

Wistaria, both purple and white.

A Few of the Best Annual Vines

Cobœa scandens, purple and white.

Moonflower, white.

Japanese Morning-glory, all colors.

Passion Flower, blue and white; must be started very early, and if well protected will sometimes survive the winter.

Japanese Gourd. This must be descended from Jonah's Gourd of biblical fame, as it often grows from forty to fifty feet in a summer. It has yellow flowers and gourds, and is very decorative.

WATER, WALKS,
LAWNS, BOX–EDGINGS, SUN–DIAL
AND PERGOLA

CHAPTER XIV

WATER, WALKS, LAWNS, BOX-EDGING, SUN-DIAL AND PERGOLA

IT is not advisable to arrange for a garden of any size without considering the question of water. Within the limits of a town supply there is only the comparatively simple matter of laying the pipes. But when the place is dependent upon its own water system, the amount to be counted upon and the situation of the garden with reference to the source of supply must be seriously considered. If possible the garden hydrants should not be more than fifty feet apart. This greatly facilitates watering. When further apart, plants are in danger of being injured by the unwieldy hose. A nozzle that will regulate the flow of water from a fine spray to a strong stream will be found convenient.

171

Opinions differ upon the best way to lay water-pipes through a place, some preferring to put them but a foot under ground, and turn off the water in winter; others lay them in trenches three and a half to four feet deep, so that they are beyond all danger from frost. This latter plan was followed in my garden and I recommend it as being most satisfactory.

The watering of a garden requires nearly as much judgment as the seasoning of a soup. Keep the soil well stirred and loose on the surface, going through the garden, where possible, with a rake; and if there is no room for a rake, stir gently with a trowel every five days or once a week. In this way moisture will be retained in the soil, since the loose earth acts as a mulch.

When watering, be generous. Soak the plants to the roots; wet all the earth around them, and do it late in the afternoon, when the sun is low. How often have I been obliged to chide the men for watering too early in the afternoon, and not doing it thoroughly, for, upon stirring the ground, I would find that the water had penetrated but a couple of inches. During long periods of dry weather, the garden, without water, will simply wither and burn.

Rhododendrons, Ferns and Lilies suffer in dry time, even though well mulched, and must be kept moist.

Japanese Iris blooms but indifferently unless quite wet.

When dry weather continues for a long period I divide the garden into three parts; one part is thoroughly watered every evening, and the following day the soil is stirred. In this way the plants suffer comparatively little. For years we had no water supply through the gardens, and really, in dry weather, life had no pleasure for me because of my unhappiness at the sight of the withered garden. I would drag watering cans about, and beg and bribe all the family to do likewise. Every afternoon, about five o'clock, one of the men would fill eight ten-gallon milk-cans with water, put them in a wagon, and drive about the place watering the flower beds and borders. Frequently he would fill these cans three times in one afternoon. This, as may be imagined, was slow and unsatisfactory work, and, except in the case of a small garden, is too great a task.

Often in a dry time, after dinner, I bethink me of the Rhododendrons or Ferns or Iris, or some other plants to which drought means death, and I feel sure "that boy has not watered them enough." Then, in ten minutes the garden skirt, shoes and gloves are on, and those thirsty plants get a drenching to their very roots such as they would never receive from any perfunctory "boy" or gardener. I go to bed warm and weary, yet sleep is sweet from satisfaction at the thought of the garden's happiness.

WALKS

Unquestionably, walks near the house should be graveled; they naturally have too hard usage to keep turf in good condition. Graveled walks should be dug out a foot or more in depth, filled in with broken stone, this covered well with coarse gravel, and finished with a coating of a couple of inches of whatever fine gravel is chosen. A walk thus made will be dry and well drained and weeds have little chance to grow.

The most beautiful walks of all are those of grass. Strange to say, they are seldom seen in this country. Through any garden, some little distance from the house, where they will be walked on only by those going to the garden, the turf-walks, with ordinary care, will last well, require only the usual cutting with the lawn-mower, and, especially if edged with Box, should be the very pride and joy of the possessor's heart.

The ground for such walks should be spaded deeply with plenty of manure, raked carefully and made very smooth. Prepare in September, and by the fifteenth or twentieth sow, very thickly, a mixture of one-third each to the bushel of Kentucky Blue Grass, Long Island Bent Grass and Red Top. Roll thoroughly, and if the weather be dry have the newly sown paths sprinkled daily and kept moist. The tender grass should appear in two weeks, and will continue to grow during October.

About Thanksgiving time of the first year, cover with a layer of straw, and uncover about the twenty-fifth of March. At this time it is well to sow thinly some more grass seed of the same kinds, and again roll, the reason for the additional spring sowing being to replace any of the grass that may have been winter-killed. About the twentieth of April spread cotton-seed meal, the best of all fertilizers for grass, all over the paths. For years we have had the lawns covered with stable manure in February and raked off the first of April, and for years I have waged war with the weeds and wild grasses. But sow cotton-seed meal early in April, and if possible give the paths a little wood-ashes in June; the result will be a hundred per cent better than from the use of manure. Cotton-seed meal should not be sown too thickly, and wood-ashes must be spread thinly, so as not to burn the grass.

The men tell me that a sharp-pointed mason's trowel is more satisfactory than any other tool for removing weeds from the lawns and grass paths. If this is carefully attended to the end of May, and again the latter part of June, and only artificial fertilizer used, there will be but little trouble with weeds in the grass.

BOX-EDGING

Box edging should be set out in the spring, that it may be thoroughly rooted before winter.

Great care must be taken in setting out the Box, that the row be absolutely straight and even. The garden cord is carefully stretched ; a shallow, narrow trench is dug with the spade, and then the little plants are placed about three inches apart, each plant against the string. The trench is half filled in with earth, then a layer of manure, and finally more earth packed down. Box planted in this way should grow and thrive, especially if given, along in May, a little bone-meal.

I write feelingly of Box edging to-day. Last week, Holy Week, I spent in the country, and most of my time was passed on my knees. For, when not at church or driving the intervening five miles, I was setting out plants in the garden, and that, like one's prayers, requires kneeling. Four men were working, setting out plants and trees, but the earth was so sweet and warm and brown that it was impossible to keep away from it. With trowel in hand and joy in my heart, I set out hundreds of little Box plants, transplanted Columbines, Foxgloves and Canterbury Bells. Big robins were hopping tamely about, calling to one another;

blackbirds and meadow-larks were singing their refrains; the brave plants were pushing their way through the earth to new life, and I thought how good it was to be alive, to have a garden to dig in, and, above all, to be well and able to dig.

With work in the garden care and worry vanish. The cook (as some cooks of mine have done) may announce that "'tis a woild waste of a place. I be lavin' the mornin'." The hamper of meat does not arrive on the one train from town, or somebody smashes something very dear to your heart,—just go to the garden, tie up some Roses or vines, or poke about with a trowel, and though murder may have been in your thoughts, in half an hour serenity will return. And what does it all matter, anyway? Another maid can cook for a few days, and there are always bacon and eggs.

Philosophy is inevitably learned in a garden. Speaking of eggs, I think of hens. Living on a farm, of course there have al-

179

ways been hens and chickens. These creatures were provided with houses and yards
and fences, and given every inducement to
remain where they belonged; yet with diabol-
ical ingenuity they would escape from their
quarters, dig under the fence, fly over it, or
some one would leave a door or a gate open,
and then, with one accord, all the flock would
make for the gardens and scratch and roll
in the borders. This sort of thing happened
repeatedly, until I felt there must be a
league between the farmer's wife and the
hens. But the limit of endurance was
reached when, one afternoon, coming out to
look at a bed of several dozen Chrysanthemums set out in the morning, I found the
poor plants all scratched out of the ground,
broken and wilted. Then in wrath the fiat
went forth, "No more hens on this farm,
those on hand to be eaten at once." For
days a patient family had hen soup, hen
croquettes, hen salad and hen fricassee, until
the last culprit came to her end.

SUN-DIAL

There is no more charming and interesting addition to a garden than a sun-dial. For hundreds of years sun-dials have been used as timekeepers, and though some of the very old ones were occasionally set into the façade of a building, they are generally found in the *plaisaunce* or garden, mounted upon quaint pedestals. Sun-dials are supposed, by their owners, to keep accurate time, but it must be remembered that there is always a difference between clock-time and sun-time. While, to-day, our lives are frequently portioned into minutes, and it would seem as if one might loiter and be lazy in a garden, if anywhere, still even among the flowers we find a "*tempus fugit.*" For a time after my sun-dial was set, it was amusing to notice how often, about half after eleven o'clock, and again at five, this late addition to the garden would claim the attention of the workmen.

181

My sun-dial stands in the center of a
formal garden where four paths meet, form-
ing a circle twenty feet across. The pedestal
is a simple column of marble, four and one-
half feet high, slightly tapering toward the
top, with beveled corners. This is placed
on a stone foundation three and one-half feet
deep, laid in cement. The pedestal I found
at the yard of a second-hand building-material
man, on Avenue B, in New York city.
After it had been set in place, I wanted it
rubbed up and a chipped place smoothed.
The only available man for this work, was
the gravestone-cutter from the nearest town.
When he was recognized at work in the
garden by passing countrymen, they supposed, of course, that some one was buried
there, and many have been the inquiries as
to "whose be that mouny-ment."

Crimson Rambler Roses twine about the
pedestal. At the corners of the four paths
are standard Box trees, which stand like
sentinels, and between them there are Bay

trees in terra-cotta vases of simple shape—
copies of antique ones.

The dial made for the latitude bears this
inscription, "*Utere praesenti, memor ultimae*"
(Use the present hour, mindful of the last),
which I found in an old book on sun-
dials in the Avery Library, at Columbia
University.

PERGOLA

Across the end of this garden is a rustic
pergola seventy feet long, made of cedar
posts cut from the woods on the farm, ten
posts on a side, each post being set four
feet deep. A string-piece of heavy chestnut
rests on the tops of each row of posts. Cedar
poles ten inches apart extend across the top
and project two feet over each side. The
pergola is eight feet wide and ten feet high,
is easy to build and very effective. Care
must be taken to set the posts at least four
feet. At each post are planted a two-year-
old root of Wistaria and one of Virginia
Creeper, and I live in the hope of some

day seeing the vines cover the pergola. The ground slopes gently where this is built, and the first autumn after it was made, it looked, from a little distance, so much like a section of an elevated railroad as to be very depressing. But one must possess imagination to be a gardener, and have the ability to see the garden as it will look "next year." So I refused to see the pergola except as clothed with vines, and in May, with the beautiful racemes of Purple Wistaria hanging from every rafter.

Patience and perseverance are traits necessary to the gardener. One must not be discouraged, but determined to succeed. If a set of plants die, or do not flourish this year, try them again next season, under different conditions, until the difficulties are overcome. I have known people who began gardening as a mere pastime when over forty years old, and who have told me what an absorbing interest it had become and how greatly it changed the whole aspect

184

of life for them in the country. What a delightful tie, fondness for gardening makes between people! I know several men with beautiful places and lovely gardens in which they take the warmest personal interest. Whenever I meet one of them at dinner, if by chance I am not seated next to him, I am unhappy and cannot listen sympathetically, either to the enthusiasm of the man on one side whose heart is, perhaps, bound up in golf, or to the laments of my neighbor on the other, who may be suffering from rheumatism or gout, and unable to eat or drink what he wants.

INSECTICIDES—TOOL-ROOM

CHAPTER XV

THE enemies of growing things have certainly increased alarmingly of late years. I cannot recall that formerly any insect was to be found in either vegetable or flower garden, other than the potato bug, currant-worm, cabbage-worm, and the green worm and small black beetle on the Rose; but now there are so many horrid creatures lying in wait until a plant is in perfection, to cut the stalk, or eat the root, or eat the pith from the stalk so that it falls, or to devour the leaves and eat the blossoms, that insecticides and a spraying machine are as necessary to a garden as a spade. For a small garden a spraying machine holding from a couple of quarts to a gallon, can be bought for a trifling sum, that will answer

189

the purpose very well. For a larger garden, a good air-pump, costing from five dollars upwards, will be found an excellent investment.

One of the best insecticides is Bordeaux mixture, which can either be bought or made. I have twenty-five gallons made at a time and keep it always on hand. The following is the receipe:

> Three pounds of blue vitriol in coarse crystals; three pounds of unslaked lime. Slake the lime in two and one-half gallons of water; pour two and one-half gallons of water over the blue vitriol in another receptacle, and let both stand over night. In the morning stir the blue vitriol until all is dissolved; then let two persons pour simultaneously the lime water and the blue vitriol into the same receptacle, and add twenty gallons of water; stir well before filling the spraying machine.

Bordeaux mixture is to be used for rust, mildew, and all kinds of blight, whenever the leaves of plants have a tendency to turn black. Hollyhocks seem to be universally attacked by rust. Spraying the plants at the end of April, and again in the middle of May, should entirely prevent this.

190

I have found that Bordeaux mixture prevents the leaves of Monkshood from turning black and falling off, if the plants are well sprayed with it about the middle of June and the first of July.

Phloxes grown in rather shady places will, in damp weather, fall victims to mildew on the leaves. Spraying with Bordeaux mixture the end of June and middle of July should prevent this. Roses also have a tendency in warm, damp weather to mildew, which can be prevented by spraying the plants with Bordeaux mixture.

Kerosene emulsion may also be prepared, and is excellent for killing, both the small green aphids that often cover the leaves of Roses, and other hard, scaly insects. Following is the receipe:

Put one cake of laundry soap shaved fine into one gallon of water. When dissolved, add two gallons of kerosene oil. This makes the emulsion.

For spraying, use one quart of the emulsion in fourteen quarts of water. Be sure that this is very thoroughly mixed before filling the sprayer.

Powdered hellebore, if dissolved in the proportion of one pound of powder to one gallon of water, will destroy both the green worm on the Rose leaf and the small dark beetle that eats the Roses. It will also dispose of green worms on other plants.

Slug-shot dissolved, one-half pound of powder to one gallon of water, will, if used the latter part of April and several times in May, keep the Roses comparatively free from insects. Slug-shot and hellebore may also be used dry and blown on to the plants with a bellows.

I have used Hellebore in my garden for many years without harm to anything except the worms and beetles. But recently I heard of a lady who was severely poisoned in using dry Hellebore. The wind blew it into her face; perhaps some was inhaled, and serious illness resulted. I mention the fact here, to caution all who use it not to let either the spray or the powder come in contact with the skin. Some persons may be susceptible to the poison while others are not,—presenting a case of what the doctors call an "idiosyncrasy."

Paris green, mixed in the proportion of two tablespoonfuls to three quarts of water and used as a spray, will destroy a beetle that sometimes appears upon the Gourd vines.

Tobacco water will kill the black aphids which appear on the stems and leaves of hardy Chrysanthemums. It will also kill green aphids. This spray is made by filling an ordinary pail lightly, not pressed down, with tobacco stems. Pour as much cold water into the pail as it will hold; let it stand for three hours, when it is ready to use in the spraying machine. This mixture will be good for only twenty-four hours.

Tobacco spray will also destroy the large red aphid (I call it this for want of, perhaps, the proper name) that has recently appeared in some localities upon the stems of the Rudbeckia (Golden Glow) and of the single hardy Sunflower, just below the blossom.

The enemy of the Box is the white spider. The insect spins its web on the Box and works from the inside. If the branches are pulled aside, the inside of the plant will be found full of dead leaves in the vicinity of the web. Recently I read in a well-known gardening monthly, that this spider could be destroyed by spraying with kerosene emulsion. I have some fine Box trees, and there were several white spider-webs on each. Watering with a very strong force of water had been tried without effect. Upon reading the article in the monthly and finding that the spider was certainly causing disaster which might be fatal, I proceeded to have the trees sprayed with kerosene emulsion, using it of the same strength as for Roses. In fact, the sprayer was not

re-filled, as there was enough left in it since
last using it on the Roses. About three
days after the Box had been sprayed, large,
unsightly brown patches appeared on the
trees, showing that the emulsion had killed
the leaves wherever it touched them. The
spider was not harmed.

I mention this experience as an example
of the danger of taking all the directions
found in horticultural publications as gospel
truth. Nor should an amateur gardener ever
be tempted to trifle with plant medicines.
I have a certain friend whose affection for
her Roses is more profound than her knowledge of how to treat their natural diseases.
Observing last summer that one of her most
cherished Crimson Ramblers was covered
with aphids, she concluded to spray it with
"something." A bottle of carbolic acid being
most available, she tested its merits at once.
The efficacy of carbolic acid as a poison
was proved beyond a doubt, for the insects
became singularly dead in a day or two, and

so did the leaves; they fell off together.
There was nothing left but the forlorn stems
and branches, looking like some freak of the
vegetable kingdom.

TOOL-ROOM

It is of the greatest importance to have
a tool-room or closet according to the size
of the place, and to require all implements
to be kept there when not in actual use.
There should be shelves across one end or
side, where shears, trowels, garden cord, clip-
pers, watering-cans, mallet, various mixtures
for spraying, oil-cans, keys for turning on
the water, twine and all the smaller things
one uses, may be found at a moment's notice.
Garden sticks painted green, in three sizes,
three and a half and four feet long, and
five-eighths of an inch in diameter, and
thicker ones an inch in diameter for Dahlias, should be kept on hand in barrels.
They can be bought of lumber-dealers
in New York, where they are known as

196

"dowels." They come in bundles of one hundred, costing from sixty cents to a dollar and twenty-five cents a bundle, according to size, unpainted, and the men can paint them on rainy days. The lawn mowers and the roller (which should be a heavy one) can also be kept in the tool-room. Rakes, both iron and wooden, hoes, spades and shovels, the latter both long-handled and short-handled, are best kept hung up along one side of the closet, where the men can see at a glance what they want.

There should also be a pickaxe and a crowbar for taking out refractory stones, and, most necessary of all things in a garden, the wheelbarrow should be kept here, too. A sickle and a scythe must not be forgotten.

If the garden is large, a two-wheel tip-cart will prove a great saver of labor in carting manure and soil and in the removal of debris.

On a particular shelf in my tool-room I

197

keep my private trowel and flower scissors, to which are attached long red ribbons as a warning of "Hands off!" to others. There is also a clipper which I often use in walking about to trim a bit here and there from a shrub or a climbing Rose.

If a scrap-book be kept, in which everything of interest pertaining to the garden can be pasted or written, it will be found a great help. In this way items about fertilizers, insecticides, special treatment of plants, with copies of lists ordered, can be preserved, and also, most interesting of all, notes of when the different plants bloom each year. I find the following under date of October 18, 1901:

> "To-day, though ice has formed three times, I have filled nineteen vases with flowers. They are Phlox, Larkspur, Monkshood, Salvia, Nasturtium, Roses, Mignonette and Chrysanthemums."

After trying many kinds of gloves for gardening, including the rubber ones, I now

use only old Suede gloves; they give sufficient covering and permit more freedom of
movement to the hands and fingers than
those of heavier material. It would be quite
impossible to transplant tiny seedlings while
wearing gloves with clumsy finger-tips.

Unless a woman possesses a skin impervi-
ous to wind and sun, she is apt to come
through the summer looking as red and
brown as an Indian; and if one is often out
in the glare, about the only headgear that
can be worn to prevent this, is the old-
fashioned sunbonnet. With its poke before
and cape behind, protecting the neck, one
really cannot become sunburned, and pink
ones are not so bad. Retired behind its
friendly shelter, you are somewhat deaf to the
world; and at the distant house, people may
shout to you and bells be rung at you, and,
if your occupation be engrossing, the excuse
"no one can hear through a sun-bonnet,"
must be accepted.

CONCLUSION

CHAPTER XVI

CONCLUSION

THE character of professional gardeners seems to be changing. They have become more perfunctory, more stubborn, more opinionated, until now it is a really serious question with them of "the danger of a little knowledge." To find a man who combines sobriety and a good disposition with a fair knowledge of his business and a real liking for it, is a difficult matter. Where but one man is kept to care for vegetables, flowers and lawn, he is more than likely to have little interest beyond potatoes or corn, or to be good at raising small fruits, and to consider everything else he has to do as so much waste of time. When first married, one of our gardeners was a German who took no interest in flowers, and planted half the vegetable garden with "kohlrabi" and "korn salad." We had never heard of these delicacies before, and did not care for them. I remember also his telling me that one kind of flower was enough to raise anyway.

If a young man with an elementary knowledge of gardening can be found, who wants to learn, is strong, willing and intelligent, it is better to supply most of the brains yourself. You will find your own wishes more apt to be carried out than by the gardener who "knows it all," and seems to resent what he calls "interference" on the part of his employer.

I remember, when a child, seeing my father's gardener walking about in the early evening after his supper, smoking a meditative pipe, tying up Roses or spraying plants, and often setting out seedlings after sundown. He was never idle; he loved his work and attended to it. But now it is rare indeed to see a gardener, after hours, going about his work; *autre temps autres mœurs.*

CONCLUSION

Remember always that it is the overcoming of the difficulties in the gardener's way, the determination to succeed, that gives zest to the occupation. Did everything planted grow and flourish, gardening would be too tame. Rust and blight, cutworms, rose-beetles and weeds, afford the element of sport so attractive to us all. A lesson must be learned from every failure; with renewed patience persevere until success is reached.

I would make the strongest plea in favor of a garden to all those who are so fortunate as to possess any land at all. The relaxation from care and toil and the benefit to health are great, beyond belief, to those who may have to work with head or hands. If you can snatch a few minutes in early morning or late afternoon, to spend among the plants, life takes on a new aspect, health is improved, care is dissipated, and you get nearer to Nature, as God intended.

If the rich and fashionable women of this country took more interest and spent more time in their gardens, and less in frivolity, fewer would suffer from nervous prostration, and the necessity for the multitude of sanitariums would be avoided.

Flower gardening is preëminently a woman's occupation and diversion. Nearly every great lady in England takes a personal interest in her gardens and conservatories, and knows all about the plants and flowers. Here, the majority of women having large places leave the direction of the flowers, as well as the vegetables and fruit, to the taste and discretion of the gardener, and thus miss a great and healthful pleasure.

As a rule, young people do not care for gardening. They lack the necessary patience and perseverance. But in the years of middle life, when one's sun is slowly setting and interest in the world and society relaxes, the garden, with its changing bloom, grows ever dearer.

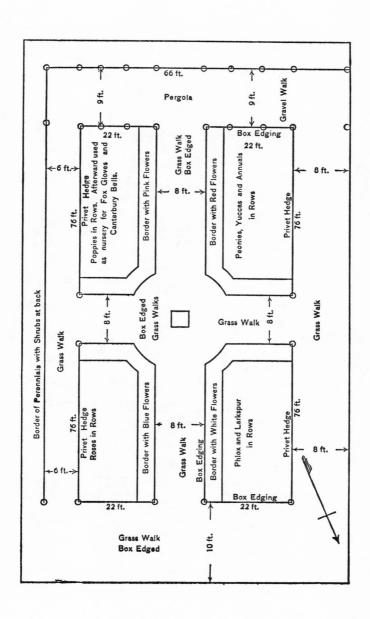

66 ft.

Pergola

9 ft.

9 ft.

Gravel Walk

Box Edging

22 ft.

8 ft.

22 ft.

Privet Hedge
Poppies in Rows. Afterward used
as nursery for Fox Gloves and
Canterbury Bells.

Border with Pink Flowers

Grass Walk
Box Edged

Border with Red Flowers

Peonies, Yuccas and Annuals
in Rows

Privet Hedge

76 ft.

76 ft.

76 ft.

6 ft.

8 ft.

8 ft.

8 ft.

Box Edged
Grass Walks

Grass Walk

Border of Perennials with Shrubs at back

Grass Walk

Grass Walk

Privet Hedge
Roses in Rows

Border with Blue Flowers

Border with White Flowers

Phlox and Larkspur
in Rows

Privet Hedge

76 ft.

76 ft.

6 ft.

8 ft.

Grass Walk

Box Edging

8 ft.

22 ft.

Box Edging

22 ft.

Grass Walk
Box Edged

10 ft.

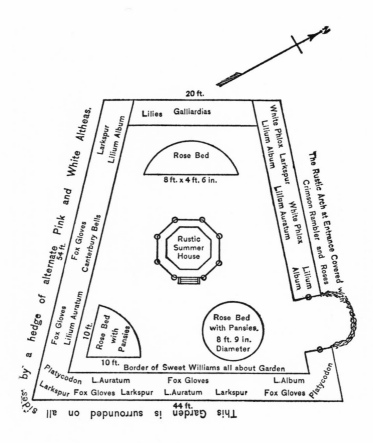

20 ft.

Lilies　Galliardias

Rose Bed

8 ft. x 4 ft. 6 in.

Rustic Summer House

Rose Bed with Pansies.
8 ft. 9 in. Diameter

Rose Bed with Pansies

10 ft.

Border of Sweet Williams all about Garden

Platycodon　L. Auratum　Fox Gloves　L. Album
Larkspur Fox Gloves Larkspur　L. Auratum　Larkspur　Fox Gloves Platycodon

44 ft.

This Garden is surrounded on all sides by a hedge of alternate Pink and White Altheas.

Larkspur Lilium Album

Fox Gloves Canterbury Bells

Fox Gloves Lilium Auratum

54 ft.

White Phlox Larkspur Lilium Album

White Phlox Lilium Auratum

Lilium Album

The Rustic Arch at Entrance Covered with Crimson Rambler and Roses

10 ft.

135 ft.

Old Stone Wall Covered with Grape Vine

Lilies　Monkshood　Phlox　Hollyhocks Lilium Candidum　Hardy Sunflowers
German Iris　Japanese Iris　Rudbeckias　Rudbeckias　Phlox　Phlox
5 ft.　7 ft.　Larkspur　8 ft.　6 ft.
Fox Gloves
12 ft.

Bed edged all the way with Sweet Williams.

PLAN FOR BORDER

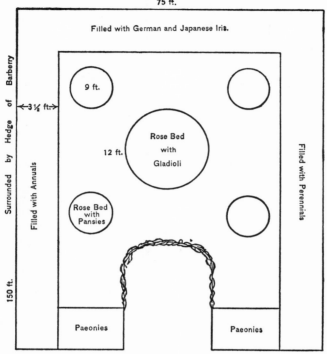

75 ft.

Filled with German and Japanese Iris.

Surrounded by Hedge of Barberry

←3½ ft.→

Filled with Annals

Filled with Perennials

150 ft.

9 ft.

12 ft.

Rose Bed with Gladioli

Rose Bed with Pansies

Paeonies

Paeonies

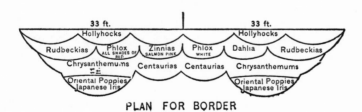

33 ft.

33 ft.

Hollyhocks

Hollyhocks

Rudbeckias

Phlox ALL SHADES OF RED

Zinnias SALMON PINK

Phlox WHITE

Dahlia

Rudbeckias

Chrysanthemums

Centaurias

Centaurias

Chrysanthemums

Oriental Poppies Japanese Iris

Oriental Poppies Japanese Iris

PLAN FOR BORDER

INDEX

Aconitum Napellus, 110.
Altheas, 160.
Ampelopsis Veitchii, 25.
Anemone Japonica alba, difficulty with, 61.
Annuals —
  List, with height, colour and period of blooming, 88.
  Sowing, 78, 80.
  Transplanting, 86.
  [*See also names of flowers.*]
Antirrhinum, sowing, 80.
Aquilegias, *see Columbines.*
Asters —
  Destruction by beetle, 14, 81.
  Sowing, 80.
Auratum lily, 139.
  Disappearance of bulb, 139.
  Price, 42.
Autumn work in garden, 70–72.
Azalea mollis, perishability of, 13.

Barberry as hedge, 51, 160.
Bedding-out plants, 120.
  [*See also names of plants.*]
Beds, rule for making, 16.
Beetle destroying asters, 14, 81.

Biennials, 117.
  [*See also names of flowers.*]
Bone-meal, 73, 74.
Bordeaux mixture, 190.
Borders —
  Around house, 29.
  Blooming from May to September, contents of border, 69.
  Planting, 29, 40–44, 67.
  Short path and narrow borders, 68.
  Small plot borders —
    Boundary lines of property, 48–50.
    Cost, 44.
    Planting, 40–44.
Boston ivy, 25.
Box, white spider pest, 194.
Box-edging, 177–178.
Bulbs, purchasing and planting, 40–44, 149–156.

Calendula, 81.
Calycanthus floridus, 160.
Campanula medium, 117.
Candytuft, planting, 46.
Cannas, 48, 120, 122.
Canterbury bells, 117, 120.

211

INDEX

Cardinal Flower, transplanting, etc., 32.
Centaurea, *see Cornflower*.
Chrysanthemums, 43, 99.
Clayey soil, lightening, 16.
Clematis paniculata, 27.
Climbing roses, 27, 131.
Columbines, 41.
  Planting, 41.
  Sowing, 93.
Coreopsis, 98.
Cornflowers—
  Blooming, etc., 81.
  Planting, 46.
Cosmos, sowing, 81.
Cost, *see Expense*.
Creepers, *see Vines*.
Crocuses, 150.

Daffodils, 41, 152–154.
Dahlias, 120, 121.
  Cost, 47.
  Planting, 45.
  Storage, 47, 48.
Delphiniums, 96.
Digitalis, 117.
Double yellow daffodils, 152–154.
" Dowels," 197.

England—
  Gardening seasons, etc., 19.
  Gardens, small plots, 37.
English ivy, 25.
Everblooming roses, 127, 134.
Evergreen shrubs, 167.
Exchange of plants, 98, 99.

Expense—
  Border planting, 40–44.
  Front beds, 47.

Fall work in the garden, 70–72.
Ferns—
  Border of, 29.
  Maidenhair haunts, 31.
  Planting, 32.
  Transplanting, 32.
  Watering, 173, 174.
Flowers—
  Annuals, *see that title*.
  Gathering, extract from English book, 77.
  Perennials, *see that title*.
  [*See also names of flowers.*]
Flower garden —
  Small plots of ground, 23, 37.
Foxgloves, 117–120.
France, small plots, 37.
Front of the house, planting bed, 45.
Funkia cærulea, 142.
Funkia subcordata, 142.

Gaillardias, 104.
German iris, 104.
Gladioli, 120, 122, 126.
  Purchasing, 43.
  Storing, 47.
Gloves for gardening, 198.
Golden Glow, 46, 47, 111.
Grandiflora, 98.
Grass walks, 175–177.
Graveled walks, 174–175.
Ground, *see Soil*.

212

INDEX

INDEX

INDEX

215

INDEX

Sweet Williams, 95.

Tigrinum, 142.
Tobacco water, 193.
Tools and tool-room, 196–199.
Transplanting—
Annuals, 86.
Cardinal flower, 32.
Fall work, 70–72.
Ferns, 32.
Perennials, 102.
Tritomas, 104.
Trumpet creeper, 25.
Tulips, 41, 150.

Unpacking plants, 65.

Valerian, 99.
Veronica longifolia, 104.
Vines and Creepers—
Ampelopsis Veitchii, 25.
Best annual vines, 168.
Care of, 25.

Vines and Creepers—
Clematis paniculata, 27.
English ivy, 25.
Henryi, 27.
Jackmani clematis, 27.
Japanese vines, 28.
North side of house, 29.
Painting of house, 25–27.
Perennials, 167.
Planting, 23.
Roses, climbing, 27, 131.
Trumpet creeper, 25.
Virginia creeper, 25.

Walks, grass and graveled, 174–177.
Water supply and watering, 171–174.
Weeding, 87.
White spider on box, 194.

Yucca filamentosa, 102.

Zinnias, varieties of, 82.

F. C.